U.K. Price
£5.50

A DOG OWNER'S GUIDE TO

TRAINING YOUR DOG

All you need to know about training your dog from puppy training to advanced obedience in the show ring

Joan Palmer

A DOG OWNER'S GUIDE TO

TRAINING YOUR DOG

**All you need to know about training your dog from puppy
training to advanced obedience in the show ring**

Joan Palmer

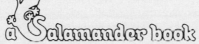

a Salamander book

**Published by Salamander Books Limited
LONDON • NEW YORK**

A Salamander Book

©1987 Salamander Books Ltd
129-137 York Way
London N79LG

ISBN 0-86101 323 9

Distributed in the UK by Hodder and Stoughton Services,
PO Box 6, Mill Road, Dunton Green, Sevenoaks, Kent TN13 2XX.

Credits

Editor: Jilly Glassborow
Designer: Stonecastle Graphics
Consultants: Harold Bellamy, Michael A. Findlay
Peter Lewis, Hal Sundstrom
Colour reproductions: TrendAdd Ltd., Essex, England and
Melbourne Graphics Ltd., London, England.
Filmset: Modern Text Typesetting, Essex, England.

Printed in Belgium

Author

Joan Palmer is a former honorary official of the National Dog Owners' Association of the United Kingdom, a voluntary organization which pioneered pet owner education and the setting up of instructors courses in dog training. She is currently a member of the Society for Companion Animal Studies, the Scottish Kennel Club and several breed clubs, and has exhibited Airedales, Chihuahuas and Chinese Crested dogs in the show ring. Other hobbies include riding, gardening, travel and historical research.

Joan has written a considerable number of full length works, including two previous dog books for Salamander. One of these, *A Dog of Your Own,* won a best Multi-Breed Book award from the Dog Writers' Association of America. A former staff journalist, Joan now works as a freelance author, writing regularly on consumer affairs and show business as well as on animal subjects. She also occasionally lectures on public relations at the School of Media Studies at the Polytechnic of Central London. Her time is divided between her London flat in Hampstead and her home in Moffat, Dumfriesshire, in Scotland.

Contents

Introduction   10

Choosing a Dog   12

Puppy Training   30

Obedience Training   38

Agility Tests and Working Trials   70

Sheepdogs and Gundogs   86

Showing Your Dog   102

Index   114

Introduction

D ogs, like children, have to be trained to conform to an acceptable standard of behaviour, and to do so they have to learn to obey commands. Once the rules have been learnt, the dogs are ready to take their place in society as man's companions, and to live full and happy lives.

The relationship between man and dog has existed since man first recognized the animal's potential as a hunter and protector. Since then, by mixing of various native types and the selective breeding of individuals, man has created a wide range of breeds to fulfil an ever-broadening range of functions.

Choosing the right dog
It would be foolish to expect a gentle gundog to take on the job of a fierce guard, or to choose a hound as a prospective obedience champion; these breeds have not been bred for

such a task. In order to avoid the disappointment of buying a dog that is not well suited for the role you wish it to fulfil, it is important first to study the various groups into which dogs are divided, according to the roles for which they were bred.

Training your dog
People that enter the world of dogs—dogdom as it is so often called—will be amazed at the diversity of interests for which the hobby caters. The countryman, for instance, may wish to train his dog to the gun, to trek or hunt with a Bloodhound pack, or even to learn the skilful art of sheepdog trialling. The town dweller, on the other hand, may wish to train his dog in basic obedience at a training class, progressing to competition level in obedience and working trials. He may, alternatively, be drawn by the excitement of competing in the show ring.

Chapter One

CHOOSING A DOG

Once the decision has been made to buy a dog, it is always tempting to rush out and buy one of the first ones you see. But buying in haste is a chancy way of finding the right canine companion. Many breeds have been bred for a specific purpose, and may therefore be accustomed to the kind of life-style which you are unable to provide. So that the breed types can easily be identified, dogs are generally divided into groups. Study of these groups will enable readers to select the dog which is most suited to their home and most able to perform the role for which it was bought, be it that of family pet, guard or obedience champion.

A small, non-aggressive dog makes a good companion for the elderly.

W hen one considers the immense time and care that most people take in selecting a house or an item of furniture, it is surprising that the family dog, which could be sharing its owners' lives for anything up to 14 years or more, is often bought on the spur of the moment. It is frequently chosen because of the breed's physical appearance rather than its character, temperament and requirements in terms of environment, exercise and feeding. Indeed, every year a lamentable number of dogs are discarded, or put down, in circumstances that could have been avoided if the owner had taken the trouble to choose a suitable animal in the first place.

You may be tempted to buy a large breed, such as an Afghan Hound or an Old English Sheepdog, but if home is an apartment, or a house with a small garden, then it would be more sensible to think in terms of a toy dog or a medium-sized dog which does not require a great deal of exercise.

If all members of a household are out at work during the day it is certainly not advisable to get a dog unless someone can return home at lunch-times to take the lonely animal for a walk; and such an arrangement is suitable only in cases of an adult dog, which is able to control the urge of nature for a reasonable time. Puppies need someone on hand during the day to feed and house-train them.

THE DIFFERENT GROUPS OF DOGS

For showing purposes the breeds are divided into a number of clearly defined groups, though these may vary from one country to another. The United Kingdom has six groups: toy dogs, hounds, terriers, working dogs, gundogs and utility dogs. The United States, on the other hand, has seven groups: toy dogs, hounds, terriers, working dogs, sporting dogs (similar to the UK gundogs), non-sporting dogs (similar to UK utility dogs) and herding dogs.

Studying these various groups (see page 172) may help you to select the dog that is most likely to meet your requirements in terms of behaviour, appearance and size.

Toy dogs

Toy dogs include breeds such as the diminutive Chihuahuas, the Affenpinscher, Miniature Pinscher, Pekingese, Pomeranian and other small pets often referred to as lap dogs, though it should be noted that the term 'toy' or 'miniature' does not necessarily imply that a dog belongs to this group; the Miniature Poodle for instance is classed as a utility breed in Britain.

The largest dogs to be found in the toy group are the Cavalier King Charles Spaniel and the King Charles Spaniel, the latter being known as the English Toy Spaniel in the United States. These attractive, friendly little dogs are an ideal choice for a family who simply wants a charming and obedient pet that will prove a reliable play-mate for the children.

Hounds

Hounds are of two distinct types; those which hunt by sight and are capable of great speed, such as the Afghan Hound, Borzoi, Greyhound, Saluki, Scottish Deerhound and Irish Wolfhound; and those which hunt by scent, such as the Basset, Beagle, Bloodhound and Foxhound.

The sight hounds will give their hearts to anyone prepared to offer them sufficient exercise and interest, though they should not be kept in cities. They have an inherent love of speed and open spaces, yet are usually obedient in the home and will lie peacefully for hours in their favourite sleeping place.

Foxhounds in the United Kingdom are the property of foxhunting packs, and they are not kept as domestic pets; as a rule it is not possible to purchase them for this purpose. The American Foxhound

---

Right: Cavalier King Charles Spaniels make excellent, obedient and good-natured companions. Neither too big or too small, they enjoy exercise without being demanding.

is exhibited in the show ring in the United States as well as being used for hunting, but is just as unsuitable for a pet as its close relative.

The scent hounds are friendly hunters with an irresistible urge to follow their noses. Members such as the Basset, the Beagle and the Bloodhound are sometimes kept as pets and are usually good with children. However, like the sight hounds, these dogs are not recom-mended for town life unless they have an energetic owner. And immense care must always be taken to prevent them escaping from the confines of a garden, which they will undoubtedly attempt to do.

Finally, it should be mentioned that hounds, although amiable enough, are not ideal for obedience work; many a wayward Beagle has driven its owner to near despair by its indifference to command.

Terriers

Terriers are busy, energetic dogs which were bred to go to ground and hunt small mammals. They are alert and loyal and would be unlikely to admit a burglar without giving noisy warning. Certainly well worth considering to perform the dual role of companion and guard would be the Airedale. It is a hardy dog and usually gets on well with children. Despite its relatively large size—the male grows up to 24in (60cm) in height—it usually adapts happily to life in town providing its owner gives it adequate exercise. This British breed was performing guard-dog duties before many other more popular breeds came into vogue, and it has never been spoilt by over-popularity.

With the possible exception of the Scottish Terrier, the Yorkshire Terrier (classified as a toy breed) and the Dandy Dinmont, a terrier's lively nature does not make it an ideal choice for an elderly person seeking a quiet, albeit affectionate, com-

panion. The terriers, especially the males, are also noted for their aggression towards other dogs, which makes them more difficult to handle than other small breeds.

Working and herding breeds

Although categorized separately in the United States, working and herding breeds are combined in a single group—working dogs—in the United Kingdom. If you are looking specifically for an obedience dog or guard dog, it is not necessary to look beyond these categories. Here one finds the German Shepherd Dog and the Border Collie, breed names which have become synonymous with obedience. Along with many other sheepdogs, such as the Belgian Sheepdog, Bearded Collie and Shetland Sheepdog, the groups also include a number of Spitz varieties, such as the Alaskan Malamute and Samoyed (a strong intelligent sled dog which benefits from obedience work and training) and, of course, the Boxer, the Mastiff and the vigilant Dobermann and Rottweiler.

Gundogs

Gundogs, or sporting dogs as the equivalent group is known in the United States, make a first class choice for buyers in search of a good-natured family pet which will also share their sporting interests. They are not natural guard dogs but are good as a warning or deterrent against burglars. The group includes the setters, pointers, retrievers and spaniels.

Utility breeds

The utility breeds (or non-sporting breeds in the United States) include dogs that have been bred for any number of purposes, such as the

Left: Jack Russell Terriers cope with lots of exercise. If allowed off the lead they may go to ground for several days.

Below: Working collies are ideal one-man dogs which tend to herd naturally. Though very intelligent, they become mischievous if bored.

Dalmatian, which was originally used for hunting in the Mediterranean countries, but was latterly used in England and France as a carriage dog. It is not only a first-class companion for anyone who wants a dog to follow a horse, but is frequently overlooked as a candidate for the obedience class in which it often works well.

Buying for security
With the unfortunate increase in crime, more and more people are looking to dogs as a form of protection. They are sensible to do

Left: A devoted pet and one of the most popular guard dogs, the German Shepherd nonetheless needs knowledgeable handling. It is happiest with a job to do and is in its element as an obedience or guard dog.

business premises against intruders. They also receive calls from elderly people, often those living alone and scared of attack, who feel that a guard dog would provide them with protection and companionship.

Many such inquirers have had long experience of dog-keeping and so understand the responsibilities involved. Others are simply looking for an animated burglar alarm, and show scant regard for the requirements of the dog. And some people do not appreciate that the perfect guard dog does not necessarily make the most suitable play-mate for their children.

The most popular guard dogs are undoubtedly the Dobermann, German Shepherd Dog and Rottweiler, all admirable and highly-intelligent breeds. However, they are, without exception, animals that need training, firm but kind handling, and space. They have an inherent restlessness, are continually on the alert, and often overguard their owners' property, even against visitors to the home.

Accidents can happen when these dogs' keen intelligence and working ability is not put to good use and the animals become bored. Also, in common with many other animals, they are quick to recognize nervousness on the part of their owners or their visitors. This nervousness may be transmitted to the dog, and a nervous dog is often a dangerous one.

Most important is that the choice of dog has the whole-hearted approval of the entire family, and that anyone who is secretly rather scared of big dogs is not presented with, say, a Dobermann as a fait accompli.

Of course, it is not always necessary to buy a traditional guard dog for a domestic situation. Mastiffs

so: it takes a stout-hearted burglar to continue with his break-in while a furious dog barks a warning of his presence. Breeders and canine societies are inundated with calls from people wanting dogs to combine the role of guard with that of family pet, or merely to guard their

GUARD DOGS

Airedale Terrier
American
  Staffordshire Terrier
  (also known as Pit
  Bull Terrier)
Anatolian
  Sheepdog
Belgian Shepherd
  Dog
Boston Terrier
Bouvier des Flandres
*Boxer
*Buhund, Norwegian
*Bull Terrier
  Bullmastiff

Collie
Corgi, Pembrokeshire
  Welsh and Cardigan
  Welsh
Dachshund
Dobermann
German Shepherd
  Dog (Alsatian)
Great Dane
Hungarian Kuvasz
*Irish Wolfhound
Japanese Akita
Komondor
Leonberger
Maremma Sheepdog

Mastiff
*Newfoundland
Puli, Hungarian
Pumi
Pyrenean Mountain
  Dog
Rottweiler
Schnauzer, Standard
  and Giant
*Scottish Deerhound
*Shipperke
Staffordshire Bull
  Terrier
Weimaraner

An asterisk denotes those breeds renowned for their reliability with children.

make formidable guard dogs as well as loyal and devoted pets. Boxers, too, are a good choice, though they are rather boisterous and tend to knock or pull small children over. In fact, it is likely that the sight and sound of any largish dog will prove a deterrent to most burglars providing it is not an obviously friendly animal.

It is unnecessary for an elderly person, who would find a large dog difficult to handle, to think that only large dogs make suitable guards. An intending burglar is unlikely to be able to determine the size of a dog by its bark, especially from the other

Below: Guard dogs at rest. Apart from the German Shepherd Dog, other breeds such as the Boxer should not be overlooked for guard work – this was originally the Boxer's prime use.

Above: The Mastiff is excellent for guarding but difficult to handle.

side of a door. Few burglars would in any case risk having their ankles bitten or their work disturbed by a snappy toy breed.

The table above shows the various breeds that make good guard dogs in the home. Those breeds that are also good with children are marked with an asterisk, but it is important to note that there are good- and bad-natured dogs in all breeds, and though the Bull Terrier, for instance, has been marked as a reliable dog with children this does not mean to say that any one individual will be trustworthy.

Dogs for obedience work

Two of the best breeds for obedience work are undoubtedly the German Shepherd Dog and the Border Collie. But should circumstances dictate that you need a smaller or less exacting pet (if, for instance, you are a town dweller) then there are plenty of other possibilities. The Shetland Sheepdog, for example, is an intelligent Rough Collie in miniature which does well in obedience work. It is happiest living in the home, rather than kennelled, and makes a good family pet.

Gundogs (sporting dogs) such as the Labrador and Golden Retrievers, the Weimaraner, the Cocker and Springer Spaniels, and even

Above: The Labrador Retriever is both an excellent gundog and a good choice for obedience work. The Yellow variety is now more popular than the Black.

members of the toy group (such as the Papillon) or the utility group (Toy and Miniature Poodles, Keeshonden, Leonbergers and Schnauzers) can also give a good account of themselves in obedience work, even though they may never reach the top. A list of dogs suitable for obedience work is shown. Again, emphasis has been placed on those breeds that are often good with children.

OBEDIENCE DOGS

Airedale Terrier	German Shepherd	Rottweiler
*Bearded Collie	Dog	Rough Collie
Belgian Shepherd	*Golden Retriever	Schnauzer
Dog	Keeshond	*Shetland Sheepdog
Border Collie	*Labrador Retriever	Smooth Collie
Bouvier des Flandres	Leonberger	Springer Spaniel
*Buhund, Norwegian	Papillon	Weimaraner
Cocker Spaniel	*Pointer	
Dalmatian	*Poodle	

An asterisk denotes those breeds renowned for their reliability with children.

Selection for the show ring

In choosing a dog for showing in the conformation ring, you must not only look for an animal with show potential and sound temperament, but also bear in mind the time you have available for its show preparation. If time is strictly limited, any idea of choosing an Airedale, Afghan Hound, Old English Sheepdog, Poodle, or any other breed that requires elaborate grooming, should be forgotten. Select a smooth-coated breed such as a Chihuahua, Boxer, Bull Terrier, Dobermann, Greyhound or Pug, all of which require comparatively little pre-show attention.

If you are keenly competitive, this must also have some bearing on the choice of breed. Classes for the more popular breeds are likely to be much larger than those for rare and less fashionable varieties, and consequently the competition is more intense. On the other hand, if you do well with an Afghan Hound, a German Shepherd Dog or a Golden or Labrador Retriever you will certainly have cause to feel pleased with yourself.

Choosing a rare breed may enable you to get into the winners and make a name for yourself in that variety. However, classes for rare breeds are limited, so it is often necessary to exhibit alongside other varieties in a special class, known, in the United Kingdom, as an Any Variety (AV) non-classified class. In the United States, such a class is known as the Miscellaneous class, which is only open for breeds designated by the Kennel Club.

Generally speaking the most sensible course for a person who is new to exhibiting is to choose a breed that, although not in the 'top twenty', is assured of good representation, and which has a fair and reasonable chance of achieving a degree of success.

In selecting a dog for the show ring you must also consider whether you require a dog or a bitch and whether you wish to have a puppy or an adult dog.

Obviously the successful show bitch is most desirable, as her line may be perpetuated. On the other hand, if you have no thought of breeding, but merely wish to have the fun exhibiting and, hopefully, owning a winning animal, you may decide on a dog. Classes for dogs are often smaller, and if the animal does well the owner can command a good stud fee.

Generally speaking, it is not a good idea to use a dog for stud work, irrespective of its pedigree, if the animal has simply been kept as a pet. It is a fallacy that pet dogs, leading a celibate life, suffer from sexual frustration. Indeed, rather than providing a pet with a service by using it as a stud, an owner could be doing himself a far greater disservice, for the dog which has mated is far more likely to urinate on the furniture and take off in hot pursuit after every bitch on heat in the neighbourhood.

Anyone choosing a dog for almost any other purpose than the show ring, should first and foremost consider buying a puppy; the earlier a puppy enters the home, the closer the bond it is likely to develop with its owner. However, with few exceptions, it is extremely difficult to pick out a prospective show-winner at six, eight or even twelve weeks; and it is usually six months, or even a year, before anyone can determine, with any degree of accuracy, whether or not a dog has show potential.

If you do wish to show your dog, but still prefer to buy a puppy, the breeder will do his best to select a promising specimen for you and, from long experience and knowledge of the breed, the chances are good that the choice will be sound. But there can be no guarantees, and in buying a pup there must always be some element of risk.

Below: Mongrels can make charming pets but their temperaments are far less predictable than those of pure breeds or crosses.

MONGRELS AND CROSS-BREEDS

Of course, when considering what type of dog to buy, many people decide against buying a pure-breed. The reasons may be charitable — it is certainly a charitable act to give a good home to an abandoned pup that has landed in a dog home or pound — or they may be financial — a mongrel is not nearly as costly a buy as a pure-breed. Unfortunately, it is because they are so cheap that they make up such a large proportion of the dogs found in dog homes and pounds; they can be acquired all too easily and, in many instances, are abandoned just as readily.

There are certain drawbacks to buying a mongrel puppy. It is not easy to know how large the adult dog will be if the parents are unknown. Nor will a buyer have any idea about the dog's temperament, such as whether it is likely to be

Above: Cross-breeds, such as this Bearded/Border Collie cross, often combine the best of both breeds.

good with children or be a natural guard. A cross-breed, on the other hand, is the result of a breeding between a dog and a bitch of known but different pedigrees and is therefore less of an unknown quantity. Again, it may not be as costly as a pure breed, but the buyer has more idea about its possible size and nature.

Many people believe that in obtaining a cross-breed they are getting the best of both breeds, and certainly many cross-breeds give a very good account of themselves in the obedience ring. However, although cross-breeds may be entered in obedience classes in the United Kingdom, only pure-bred dogs may compete in obedience in the United States.

It is worth noting that there is no truth in the commonly held belief that mongrels and cross-breeds are more intelligent than pure-breeds.

But, as pets, they are just as loyal and affectionate as their pedigree comtemporaries. It is true to say, however, that both mongrels and cross-breeds may be less likely to suffer from the various hereditary complaints which afflict many pure breeds of dog.

BUYING YOUR DOG

Whether pure-bred or mongrel, puppies should ideally be selected while still with their littermates, using two main criteria—health and temperament.

Avoid puppies which have evidence of coat staining from diarrhoea or vomiting, those with dirty eyes or ears, and those with any patches of hair loss.

As an indication of further temperament, you should also avoid puppies that isolate themselves from the other littermates, and those that retreat in response to a sudden noise such as a hand-clap, or the dropping of a large bunch of keys. The better puppies will regard such provocation with interest and will want to investigate the cause.

Adult dogs acquired from dog homes, animal charities and breed rescue organizations should be subjected to the same general health checks as puppies. However, they may have been rejected by the owners because of some inherent vice, such as biting humans, aggression towards dogs or other livestock, over-sexedness or indoor incontinence, and these can rarely be spotted by a cursory glimpse.

Sale or return

Acquisition or purchase of a new dog or puppy should be subject to a health clearance by a veterinarian. If for any substantial reason the animal is found to be unfit, it should be (and is, by law, in the United Kingdom) returnable to the source for a full refund of any monies paid, providing a veterinary certificate is produced stating clearly the reason for rejection, and providing this is done within a reasonable time of acquisition—say, seven days.

Similarly, adult dogs acquired from sources as stated above should have a seven or fourteen day 'warranty' which should allow a

return and refund if any vice is discovered which renders the animal unacceptable to the new owner. Most organizations involved with dog rescue not only volunteer this, but insist on this as a condition. The reason, of course, is to stop the highly undesirable practice of 're-cycling' unsatisfactory dogs from one home to another, possibly involving maltreatment and certainly unsettling and causing unhappiness to the dog.

Where to go

Having decided what type of dog you want and the role you wish it to fulfil, be it that of guard, companion or show champion, there may be several options open to you with regards to where to buy your pet.

In the case of almost every recognized breed of dog there exists a relevant breed society, or breed club as it is known in the United States. Each society liaises with the national kennel club in matters appertaining to its breed, holds regular events, and generally assists members in all matters relating to the breed. If you decide to buy a pure-breed, a request to the relevant club or society will bring forth addresses of reputable breeders. (The national kennel club will help you contact the breed club.)

You may, of course, have to travel some distance to find the breed of dog you require, particularly if it is a rare one. You must also be prepared to go some distance if you live in a town: with the exception of breeders of small dogs, most breeders tend to live in rural areas. You will need to give the breeder a full description of the type of dog you are looking for; for example, whether you want a dog that is bred from a long line of working stock, or if you want a promising show prospect which you can actively campaign. And bear in mind that with dogs, as with most other things, you only get what you pay for. A puppy with some slight defect as far as coat, colour, size or some other show fault is concerned, may not cost as much as a more

Below: Ideally, puppies should be selected while still with their littermates.

perfect specimen, but then neither will it be of show standard.

Breeders pride themselves in their kennels' reputation and their wins in the show ring, so they tend to be very choosy about the people to whom they sell their most likely prize-winners, regardless of the amount of money they may be offered. If you do wish to show your pet, it is important to convince the breeder that you are keen to succeed and will make a caring owner. Providing you do this, the breeder should do his or her very best for you, as well as give endless help and advice.

Most breed societies or clubs operate a breed rescue scheme, whereby any misplaced breed member is housed by a representative of the society pending a suitable home being found for it. In the United States, the Humane Society also has many shelters which care for misplaced dogs. Dogs find their way into rescue schemes for any number of reasons — they may be the victim of a broken home, bereavement or simply an

Below: Homes for unwanted dogs are an ideal source for a new pet, but beware of problems. Have a vet check the pup soon after acquisition and allow a settling-in period to confirm your choice.

Above: New puppies need special attention having just left the litter. In addition to warmth and food they need much companionship to establish them in their new home.

unwanted pet—and such schemes provide an ideal source for the buyer who is not looking for show stock and does not mind giving a home to an older dog, providing it is of the desired breed.

It must be remembered that, although breed rescue schemes try to find out as much as they can about a dog's background, there may be some element of risk in buying a dog about which little or nothing is known. The same, of course, applies to buying a mongrel or any other dog from a dog home or pound.

A reputable pet store will probably be able to obtain the pure-breed of your choice providing it is not too rare. However, if you are considering showing, the chances of such a dog conforming to its breed standard are slender. It is more likely to be a sub-standard specimen, such as the runt of a litter, which the breeder has passed on to the dealer in the hope that it will find a good home. Such an animal can make a healthy and attractive pet but is unlikely to be a show-winner.

If you are prepared to take a chance with buying a mongrel, bearing in mind that you will have little or no idea of how it will grow up with regards to size, appearance and temperament, then you may find what you want either advertised in the local paper, in a pet store or in a dog home or pound.

Chapter Two

PUPPY TRAINING

A dog's formal training does not usually begin until it is six months of age, but prior to this time there are still many lessons to be learnt. First and foremost, a young puppy must be taught to perform its toilet in the correct place. It must also learn to respond to its own name, to learn where to sleep at night, and to become accustomed to wearing its collar and lead. At this stage, it is also important to begin training a puppy to become accustomed to traffic. Before your dog is six months, it is worth investigating the dog training classes that are available in the area, and to begin preparing it for its formal obedience training.

Early lead training should be given at home before taking a pup onto the street.

Tempting though it may be to permit a puppy to do as it wishes, training—in easy stages—is essential. Dogs are pack animals accustomed to the dictates of a leader. In any situation where a number of dogs are kept, such as in breeding kennels, it is easy to define the 'boss' dog from which the others take a lead, and to mark out its likely successors. In a domestic environment the companion dog looks to its human master for authority and leadership. A well trained dog is therefore a 'happy' dog, and is not only a pleasure to its handler, but can also be a pleasure to other people who have to share its environment.

Naming your dog

It is important to give your puppy a name before progressing with its training; your dog must be familiar with its name so that it is left in no doubt, when you issue a command prefaced by 'Bob', 'Jet' or 'Nell', that you are referring to it. Try to avoid fancy names containing several syllables and restrict your choice to those such as Ben, Moss, Jill, Red and others which are easy to deliver—and for the dog to recognize. You should then use the chosen name whenever you refer to the dog: 'Good boy Ben', 'Shall we take a walk now, Ben?'.

We have all heard proud owners remark that their dog understands every word they say. Dogs cannot, in fact, understand the meaning of words but they do associate sounds with actions, so that the dog told to get its 'lead', come and have its 'dinner', or go to 'bed', soon associates the emphasized, often repeated, word with an action or event.

House-training

House-training, or house-breaking as it is called in America, should begin almost from the moment the puppy arrives in its new home. It is vital for the owner to understand that some dogs—and indeed certain breeds—have a higher intelligence quotient than others and that, even in the matter of toilet training, one puppy may learn in a fortnight what it could take another several months to grasp. However, the slowest of learners may eventually turn out to be the cleanest of dogs.

You cannot put your puppy in its basket at night and expect it to be clean until morning. Puppies cannot control the urge of nature as long as adult dogs, nor should they be expected to do so. But by carrying out the following steps it should be possible to house-train your puppy as speedily, and with as little upset, as possible.

Having positioned the basket in a draught-free place, cover the surrounding floor area with newspaper. Place the puppy onto the paper after each drink, or meal, praising it lavishly when it performs its toilet. You should also put the puppy onto the paper after each mishap or when it is preparing to evacuate elsewhere. The circling movement of a pup about to squat will soon become easy to recognize.

Once the puppy has learnt what the paper is there for, the paper should be moved close to the door which leads into the yard or garden. When the puppy has got into the habit of toddling to the door you can open it and encourage the pup to perform its toilet out of doors. Before long the puppy will stand at the door whenever it wants to be let out. You should also put the puppy out for a few minutes after each meal or drink, and first thing in the morning and at bed-time.

The owner without a garden, or yard, has a more difficult problem, particularly as, on no account, should the pup be allowed to venture out into the street until after its routine inoculations have taken effect. In such circumstances, newspaper should be laid as before, and the pup should be encouraged to perform its toilet in a cat litter tray.

Always praise lavishly when your puppy has performed in the correct place, uttering the words 'Good boy' (or 'girl') and, most importantly, the pup's name. The puppy wants only to learn, and to please you.

An owner should never resort to slaps, or the unhygienic habit of

Above: A sternly voiced reprimand combined with a pointing finger is enough to let this Beagle pup know that it has done something wrong.

Below: This pup should be praised for learning so young to relieve itself outdoors and on the grass border — a first step to kerb training.

rubbing the pup's nose in its own faeces when there has been a mishap. Tone of voice should be sufficient admonishment.

Bed-time

It is a mistake to allow a small pup to snuggle down at the foot of your bed in the belief that, in a week or two, it can be transferred to its designated quarters. If you take this course of action the pup, once dismissed to the kitchen (or kennel) will constantly endeavour to be reinstated at close proximity to you. You would also be performing a disservice to the pup. If it can attain a degree of independence this will prove beneficial should you, at some future date, have to leave it in the care of another person, or in boarding kennels.

When the time comes to say 'Goodnight', you must do so firmly, but gently. First make sure that there is nothing in the room against which the pup could fall and injure itself, or that it might chew, then lay the puppy gently in its bed and tuck a warm, hot water bottle under the bedding. This will provide comfort and warmth similar to that which the pup derived from its mother and litter brothers and sisters. You may also like to tuck a small alarm clock into the basket — the puppy will associate the ticking with the beating of its mother's heart, and this will help to comfort it. Then, having left a bowl of water within close proximity, say 'Goodnight' firmly, and put out the light.

You may not hear a whimper until morning. More likely, if the puppy has been receiving a lot of attention it will, on finding itself deserted, set up a plaintive howl. If you must rise from your bed, lift a finger to your mouth very sternly as you warn the puppy to 'be quiet'. Do not give in or return a second time. Once a ritual has been established, the puppy will soon reconcile itself and stay peacefully in its own bed until morning.

Early lead training

Although the pup must not be taken out into the street until its inoculations have taken effect, the early weeks present a good opportunity for the owner to accustom it to wearing a collar and lead.

You should start by using a soft collar and lead, making sure you do not fasten the collar too tightly — as a rule there should be enough slack to enable you to slip two fingers beneath the collar. Let the pup toddle about wearing the collar and lead for short periods of time, taking care that is does not trip up or get the lead caught on anything.

Once the puppy has learnt to accept the collar and lead, you can begin to accustom it to positioning itself by your side. You can do this by placing the puppy well in front of you and offering it a treat in your left hand. Then, holding the lead in your right hand you should draw the puppy gently towards you, saying 'Good boy' (or 'girl') as you do so. Once the pup is readily coming to your left hand side, you can move gradually backwards, increasing the space the pup must cover to reach you. Soon you will be able to revert to leading the puppy on your left hand side in preparation for teaching it to walk at heel.

Dog training clubs

Many people decide to enrol their puppy at a dog training class. However, it is unusual for such clubs to accept puppies under six months of age and, as there may be a waiting list, it is a good idea to make contact with a local club as soon as possible and perhaps to attend a training session as a spectator.

It is important when choosing a club to find one which operates in line with your special interest and that you do not enrol at a dog training club if what you are really looking for is a ringcraft class, better known as a showing or handling class in the United States.

Training clubs specialize in teaching basic obedience, in some cases progressing to competitive obedience and agility. The ringcraft class, on the other hand, prepares new entrants for the show ring.

The breed enthusiast who wishes to exhibit in the show ring will usually find the breed society knowledgeable about clubs within a reasonable

Above: Even at an early age before starting its formal training, a puppy being walked in town must be kept on the lead at all times. It should be given gutter-training and will eventually become accustomed to traffic and distractions that might be encountered on an every day outing.

radius that offer ringcraft training. However, such clubs are not as abundant as dog training clubs. It is sensible to check out the facilities offered by the various local clubs with the local reference library, the veterinarian's surgery or with local dog breeders or boarding kennels.

It is important to note that trying to combine both show ring and obedience training is not always satisfactory. The show dog, for instance, is required to stand for lengthy periods in the ring, whereas the obedience dog is more accustomed to remaining in a sit or down position. Such differences can prove confusing for a young dog.

Some dog training clubs are affiliated to the national kennel club, others are privately owned. Recently, in some countries, such as the United Kingdom, clubs have been set up under the auspices of the local authorities who are anxious to promote pet owner education and canine care.

Most dog training clubs are, first and foremost, concerned with basic obedience, and teaching a dog to 'sit', 'stay', 'come' and 'heel'. Whether those who take advantage of the facilities will progress to competitive obedience must depend on the extent of their ambition, whether they have the right dog (in terms of breed and capability), on the club facilities, and on the experience of the instructors concerned.

Clubs obviously differ in what they have to offer and the length of the courses, but the following is an indication of what you may expect from an average club.

The club may offer an introductory course (lasting about eight weeks) which concentrates on solving problems, teaching basic exercises and enabling pupils to get to know the temperament of their dog.

The next stage would involve more heelwork, introduce hand signals, prepare for handling off leash, and teach the retrieve. Follow-

Above: At a training class dogs are made to sit, with their owners in attendance ready to discourage distractions from neighbouring dogs.

Left: These dogs are learning to sit-stay. During this exercise they are expected to obey commands without distraction from neighbours.

ing this, the more advanced stage would give instruction on send aways and more serious obedience work. Owner and dog would not be put into a higher class level, simply because they have attended the club for a specific number of weeks, until they have mastered the preliminary exercises.

When pupils attend class for the first time they may be given a problem sheet which lists various difficulties that can be encountered with a new pet, such as jumping up at people, barking excessively, and showing aggression towards other dogs. Attendants would be asked to tick the faults which apply to their dogs, so that individual attention can be given to their needs.

Chapter Three

OBEDIENCE TRAINING

Once it is old enough, every dog should be taught to respond to the basic commands of 'sit', 'down', 'come', 'stay' and 'heel'. In certain circumstances instant obedience to one of these commands may save a dog's life, particularly where collision with a car seems imminent.

But formal training need not stop with the basics. There are many more advanced exercises which a dog must learn if it is to compete in exciting sports such as obedience trials. These include scent discrimination, retrieve, and the 'down-stay' for up to 10 minutes duration. It is up to the owner to decide how far he or she wishes to progress with the training.

Formal obedience training usually begins when the dog is about six months of age.

In obedience training the handler must remember from the start that, to the dog, every exercise it is taught is another game. The mind of the dog is such that it is always striving to please its handler but as soon as the enjoyment factor goes out of training, and the game becomes a bore, the dog will lose its enthusiasm to learn and will start to misbehave.

The dog — rather like the small child who quickly tires of lessons — finds it hard to concentrate for long. Therefore, it is important that initial training sessions do not extend beyond five minutes. You can ensure that the dog has not forgotten what it has been taught by commanding it to sit at various times during the day. And, when it is playing in the garden and brings back its ball, remember that it is actually learning how to retrieve.

Equipment

During training the owner should use a 6ft long (1.8m) lead made either of leather or nylon. A 'safe' collar, usually a check chain, should also be worn by the dog at all times.

A check chain is a length of chain with a small ring at each end. To use it, you must double part of the chain through one of the rings to form a noose. Facing the dog, the noose should be slipped over the dog's head and the free ring attached to the leash. It is important that the noose is correctly positioned on the dog as otherwise it will not be effective. A correctly fitted check chain serves two purposes — it com-

Below: Most dogs will get great fun and good exercise chasing and retrieving toys such as this ring.

Above: To fit a check chain, form a noose with the ring-loop hanging down. With the dog walking on your left, the chain will operate correctly.

Below: This chain is fitted incorrectly; it will not slacken when released and may choke the dog.

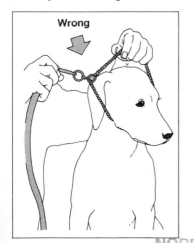

Wrong

bines comfort for the dog with control for the handler. (For correct positioning of the chain see photograph above.)

The ring through which the chain passes must be free to slide up and down the chain, so that when the leash is raised the noose tightens and when the leash is lowered the noose immediately slackens. The chain must also be long enough to ensure proper sliding action, but there must be no more than 4in (10cm) spare when the chain is tight around the dog's neck.

To use the chain correctly, you should apply a forward guiding movement as you gently bring the dog up from the sit position and into forward motion. This action must be simultaneous with the word of command 'heel'. The action of the collar tightening round the dog's neck on the forward movement of the lead, and its release upon the dog obeying the command and moving with the handler, teaches the dog to obey commands promptly.

Where to start

You should begin to train your dog in earnest when it is six months old. The following are a few points worth noting before you start.

Who should train? One person should be responsible for training a dog, but all family members should be encouraged to take an interest.

Consistency Being consistent in the issuing of commands is vital. It will confuse the dog if one family member uses the command 'sit', while another uses the words 'sit down'. The table lists the most common words of command and their meanings.

How often and how long? In order to train your dog properly you must be prepared to set aside a certain amount of time. Generally speaking, five-minute sessions given four times a day, or even two 10-minute sessions, are quite sufficient.

Home work Some dog training clubs give their pupils home work, with goals to be attained each week.

Where to train During initial training it is best to practise in an area familiar to the dog, and free from distractions, such as in the garden. Later training can be undertaken with distractions.

How to end the lesson A lesson should always end with a short play session, with the dog on the leash so that the owner still maintains physical control.

Wearing apparel Owners should avoid wearing tight-fitting clothes for dog training, and women should not wear high heeled shoes. Preferably, you should wear comfortable clothes and flat shoes or trainers.

Smoking People should not smoke while training their dogs.

Praise Throughout the lessons, and indeed for the remainder of your dog's life, the animal should be praised, using the word 'good' —

'good boy', 'good girl', 'good dog'. By the tone of voice the words should be made to sound sincere and meaningful.

Petting Verbal praise and encouragement is essential to training, but any physical expression of praise distracts a dog from its lessons. This is better left until after the successful performance of an exercise.

Nagging You should not nag your dog by continually repeating a command, for example, by saying 'sit, sit, sit'. You are virtually asking your dog to sit on the third command. Give a clear command to your dog, once only. If the dog does not obey a first command you should apply correction by repeating the command, and at the same time giving a physical demonstration of what the dog should be doing.

Know your breed Most novice dog owners tend to read up as much as they can on their chosen breeds. They should, therefore, know what their dog was bred for and utilise this knowledge in its training. For example, the Labrador Retriever should be exceptionally good at retrieving, the Shetland Sheepdog at heelwork and the Basset Hound and Beagle at following a scent.

Words of command

Come	Come to me
Down	Lie down
Heel	Walk on my left side
Okay	A release word meaning 'You can move now'
Sit	Sit down
Stand	Stand up
Stay	Remain in position

Right: Many people use a traditional check chain and leather leash for training. A good alternative is the nylon head collar designed by British canine behaviourist Dr Mugford which can be used in conjunction with a retractable leash.

TRAINING YOUR DOG

The following instructions outline simple and effective methods of training your dog to obey your commands. The initial commands ('sit', 'stay', 'heel' and 'down') are an essential part of basic training which all pet owners should teach their dogs to obey. The more advanced obedience exercises are those which a dog must master if ever it is to be entered into obedience trials.

It is important to point out that just as one trainer may prefer to use a nylon collar and canvas lead, and another a traditional check chain and bridle leather leash, there is more than one way of training a dog. The best way is to begin by using a tried and trusted method and then, perhaps, as you advance, start to become a little more adventurous, finally settling on a combination of methods.

One of the things that will quickly be discovered is that most obedience exercises performed in trialling are merely an extension of those learnt in the preliminary stages, the main differences being that, as training progresses, these exercises will be executed with and without distractions, both on and off the lead, and on different surfaces.

It will be appreciated that a handler working a dog off the lead has a far less degree of physical control,

therefore, the basic exercises must be completely mastered on lead before proceeding to a higher level.

Obedience training is a logical progression from one exercise to another. Timing is very important. While each exercise must be fully grasped before another is commenced, most exercises can be broken down into parts and introduced as part of normal play before formal training begins.

Sit

To teach the dog to sit you should start by holding the lead in the right hand — a dog is always taught to sit on the left hand side of its handler. Then, with your left hand, press the dog's hindquarters down, at the same time giving the command 'sit' in a firm voice. You should always keep your back straight while performing this, so as not to bend over the dog in case this intimidates it.

Once the dog has learnt what is required, it should be praised lavishly and may be rewarded with a titbit. In time the dog will learn to sit promptly on command without a lead being used.

Teaching the Sit

1 *On the command 'sit', press the dog's hindquarters firmly down with your left hand while keeping the dog's head supported in the air.*

2 *Keep the lead taut in the right hand, giving it a slight upwards pull as you press the hindquarters down to help the dog respond.*

3 *Crouching down beside, but not over, the dog may prove helpful in teaching more unruly dogs to perform the exercise correctly.*

Sit-stay

To teach the sit-stay, command the dog to 'sit' and, holding the lead in your right hand, move a pace to the right, watching out for any sign of movement in the dog. If the dog is unsteady, return to it and repeat the command. If it is steady, back away to three-quarters of the length of the lead, giving the command 'sit-stay' as you do so. Under no circumstance should you allow the lead to become tight as this will cause the dog to get up. Remain at a distance for a short period of time, initially perhaps counting up to five, then walk back to the dog and fondle and praise it. Whilst away from the dog you should not speak or move unnecessarily.

As training progresses, you will be

Left: In obedience training a dog is always taught to sit on the left hand side of its handler.

able to extend the length of time your dog is required to sit-stay, and eventually the lead will no longer become necessary.

Heelwork

With the dog walking beside you on the left hand side, you should give a slight jerk on the check chain and use the command 'heel boy' ('heel girl') whenever the animal gets in front of you. This will have the effect of tightening the collar, causing the dog to fall back into place beside you. The dog must be kept close to your left thigh, and turns should not be attempted until the dog is competent at walking at heel. Nor should the exercise be attempted off the lead until perfected.

During heelwork it is important to give praise or otherwise at the right moment. Encouragement should be given while the dog remains at heel but if you have to correct the animal by use of the check collar,

2 Then move in front of the dog jerking on the check chain if any attempt is made to move. If the dog does move, start again.

Teaching the Sit-stay
1 Put the dog in the sit position by holding your hand up in front of its face and giving the command 'sit' in a firm voice.

Walking to Heel

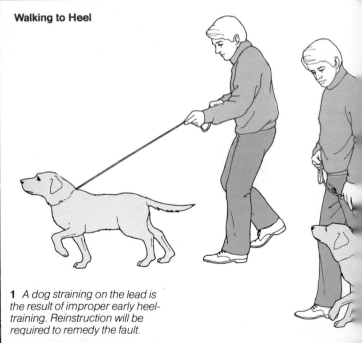

1 A dog straining on the lead is the result of improper early heel-training. Reinstruction will be required to remedy the fault.

3 Keeping your hand high up in front of the dog, and repeating the command 'stay', back off bit by bit, increasing the space between you.

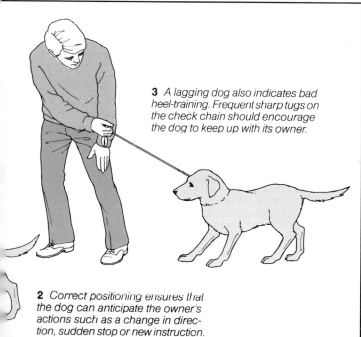

3 A lagging dog also indicates bad heel-training. Frequent sharp tugs on the check chain should encourage the dog to keep up with its owner.

2 Correct positioning ensures that the dog can anticipate the owner's actions such as a change in direction, sudden stop or new instruction.

Teaching the Down-stay

1 *Teach the dog the down position by sliding the dog's front legs forward and pushing the shoulders firmly down towards the ground.*

2 *The 'down-stay' command is then given to emphasize the position. Keep repeating it and try to avoid too much repetitive pushing down.*

then at that moment your tone of voice should indicate displeasure. It should not be necessary to use more than a dog's name and the command 'heel', the tone of your voice should do the rest.

Down

There are several ways to teach your dog the 'down' command. One is to get it to sit at your side, and then gently slide its front feet forward until it attains the down position, remembering as you do so to give the command 'down' in a clear, positive voice, and praising the dog when it has successfully accomplished the exercise for you.

Another method of getting the dog down is to put it in the sit position at your side, and for you to go down on one knee with your left hand against the dog's shoulder. The right hand then removes the dog's left foot from the ground whilst pressure from the left hand pushes the dog down sideways. This should be performed with the simultaneous command of 'down'.

For many, the easiest way to get the dog down is to pass the lead under the left foot, holding the lead in the right hand. By pulling the lead and pushing down on the dog's

back at about shoulder level with the left hand, and giving the command 'down', the dog should go into the required position.

The command 'down' is an extremely important one to teach your dog, as instant observation to this command can sometimes avoid traffic accidents, for example, when a dog is on the point of dashing across the road in front of an oncoming vehicle. Such incidents can not only mortally injure the dog but can also cause loss of human life if the vehicle swerves to avoid the dog and, instead, crashes into another car or pedestrian.

Down-stay

This exercise can be taught once the dog has mastered the 'down'; having achieved the down, emphasis must be placed on the word 'stay', so that the command becomes in effect 'down-stay'.

The procedure is taught in exactly the same manner as the 'sit-stay', the handler backing off a few paces then returning to praise the dog, gradually increasing both the distance and the time spent away from the dog. At first you may perform this exercise with the dog on a long lead laid out on the floor between

3 *When settled in the down position repeat the command 'stay' and reinforce this by giving a hand signal in front of the dog's face.*

The down-stay sequence is an extension of the sit-stay routine. Practise it till it becomes second-nature—this usually takes 3-4 days.

you. But do remember that you must return to correct the dog each time it moves. Ultimately, the lead will not be required.

Recall

Most owners of young dogs have witnessed, often with something approaching helplessness, the sight of their puppy chasing round and round in circles after an outing, refusing to be caught or have its lead put on, and frequently making the owner look ridiculous.

When the wayward dog is finally captured the natural reaction may be to reprimand it severely. Yet such treatment, especially if repeated on a number of occasions, is likely to have the reverse effect, for the dog will associate the action of returning to its handler with that of a reprimand. The whole essence of training is based on love, praise and reward. If, when the dog finally returns, it is praised, the action will have a pleasurable association.

To teach this exercise the 'sit' and 'down-stay' must first be mastered. Then, using the command 'sit' followed by the command 'wait' you should back away from the dog to the extent of the lead, being careful not to pull the lead tight until you

command the dog to 'come'. The command should be given in an inviting tone encouraging the dog to come quickly to you. The command 'sit' should be given as the dog arrives in front of you and this may be reinforced by pushing the dog into the sit position with the left hand.

Should the dog anticipate the command of 'come', you must not make too much of this otherwise problems may arise later. Take the dog back quietly and give it a firm command of 'sit'.

For competitions emphasis should be made here of the importance of getting the dog to sit straight in front of the handler. Care should be taken not to handle the dog too much in doing so as this is likely to be counter-productive. Instead, you should take half a pace back with one foot and guide the dog into the space created, the other foot acting as a guide for the dog, thereby encouraging it to sit straight.

Down, out of sight

Once your dog has mastered the 'down-stay' you may like to issue the command while you slip out of sight for a few moments, remembering as you do so not to speak or look directly at your dog, or give any sign or movement simiiar to the action of doing the recall.

Your dog will eventually learn to 'down-stay' for considerable periods of time. Indeed, once you begin to take its response for granted you could, if you are not careful, forget that your well trained dog is still 'on command'. On return to your dog you should use a chosen 'release' word to cancel out the command to stay. Such a word should only be used for the purpose of releasing the dog from a previous 'stay' command, and only given when you return to the dog's side.

Sit-finish

One of the achievements that most impresses the obedience enthusiast is the way in which an obedient dog will, on completion of an exercise, return to its handler on command, do a straight 'sit' in front of him, and go quietly round the handler's legs to the heel position when that command to do so is given.

The dog will already have been taught to sit in front of its handler during the recall. Now it must be taught to go to heel on the handler's command from the sit in front. This can be taught as follows.

With your dog sitting in front of you and the lead in your right hand, give the command 'heel' and draw the right hand back behind you, gently drawing the dog round. Passing the lead behind you into your left hand, guide the dog round on to your left side and give the command to sit. This must be done gently and with much encouragement.

Sit on heel

The purpose of this exercise is to teach your dog to sit whenever you stop walking, for instance, when you stop to cross the road. At first your dog will not be accustomed to being commanded to sit while waiting at heel, though it will already have been taught to sit on command at your side. When the sit is incorporated into heelwork there should be little problem, though it may be necessary to go back to guiding the dog for a while, by raising the lead in the

right hand and pushing the dog's hindquarters into a sitting position. Soon the dog will be sitting automatically when the handler stops.

Retrieve

Formal training for the retrieve can begin only when the recall is being performed reliably. Preparation can begin in play by getting the dog interested in fetching a variety of articles. Care must be taken to select articles which will build up the

dog's confidence. In other words, you should not expect the dog to pick up any item which is too large, too heavy or awkward.

The exercise should be started with the dog sitting by your side. Offer it a stick, a dumb-bell, or any particular article that the animal has shown interest in fetching and carrying. If the dog takes the article from you, you should praise it lavishly. Keep repeating this part of the exercise. Now hold the article

Above: Police dogs are taught the 'down, out of sight' exercise, during which they must not move until 'released' by their handlers.

just below the dog's chin and instruct the animal to 'hold'. If the command is obeyed, again praise lavishly before taking the article away.

Next, you should keep lowering the article until it is picked up from your hand at floor level, then, by

51

stages, from the floor itself at distances of up to a yard away.

If work on the sit-stay and recall has been done thoroughly, you should now be able to command the dog to 'wait' while you throw the article a short distance and then to 'fetch'. On its return the dog should be asked to 'sit' in front of you so that the article can be taken from it. The animal must then be praised for an exercise well done.

Below: In the retrieve, the dog sits while the dumb-bell is thrown, and is then encouraged to 'fetch' by the handler pointing to the object.

Above: Having fetched the dumb-bell, without chewing it, the dog must sit in front of the handler, offering the article until it is taken.

Scent

To perform this exercise a dog must be taught to retrieve an article from amongst other similar articles by means of scent alone. It follows that the retrieve must be well practised before scent discrimination is attempted.

You can start the training by finding an article which is acceptable to the dog, perhaps the same item that you used when teaching the retrieve. Carry this item on your person for about a week, so that it is well scented, then place it on the floor with one or two well-washed, and unscented articles. To avoid scent contamination of the un scented articles they should be kept in clean polythene bags until the exercise begins, and then tipped straight onto the floor.

Take the dog up to the articles and, starting with those which are unscented, command the dog to 'seek'. Encourage the dog to examine each item, and to pick up that which is scented. Once this has been achieved the item should be taken from the dog, and the animal praised.

· Once you are satisfied with the dog's performance 'on-lead', you can proceed to send the dog to seek 'off-lead', making sure, at all times, that the requisite article is well scented. Practice will increase the dog's confidence so that you may gradually increase the number and

type of articles displayed. When the exercise is going well you can occasionally practise with cloth articles in preparation for advanced competition work. In such competitions articles provided by the judge will be used. These vary enormously so your practice items must include a wide range of materials.

Advanced scent competitions vary from country to country. Typically, however, the dog must find an article, with the judge's scent on it, from a total of 10 articles. This is not an easy task, especially as false scents by other people will be included.

Send Away

This is an exercise which can be started in play at a fairly early stage; however, you will need a friend to assist you. Ask the friend to walk about 10ft (3m) away and call the dog by name. Now release the dog, giving the command 'away'. The friend should praise the dog for obeying the command, and you should do likewise to boost the dog's confidence.

In formal training the send away is taught by using an article, or marker, with which the dog is familiar, such as a piece of its bedding. Place the article on the ground and, starting from about 6ft (1.8m) away, give the command 'away' and guide the dog, on the lead, to the article. On reaching it, give the command 'down'. The dog should then be praised and the exercise can be repeated. This time you can move back to about 10ft (3m). When the exercise has been successfully repeated, you should start again, at the shorter distance, sending the dog 'away' off the lead. You must always set the dog facing towards its ultimate destination using both hands to point the dog's head towards the area where the article lies.

The distance can be lengthened by stages, moving the marker to different locations, all the while building up the dog's confidence in going away until eventually you are able to add the command 'down' subsequent to recall.

Distant Control

This is a fairly advanced exercise which, in competition work, typically consists of the dog obeying six commands given by the handler at the judge's instruction.

To perform the exercise the dog must obey the commands 'down', 'sit', and 'stand' promptly. The exercise has to be carried out from a distance of not less than 10 paces and the dog must not move forward in the carrying out of the commands. Therefore, the dog must be taught to obey the various commands while remaining on the spot.

Training should start by teaching the 'sit to the down', as already described on page 122. It is important to get the dog doing this movement without stepping forward or shuffling to one side, and the best teaching method to use is the one in which you put your left foot over the lead near to the dog's shoulder and take the strain on the lead. You must practise this exercise before moving on to the next stage, but 'make haste slowly' — you must not let the dog get bored with any stage of the exercise. The dog must be given much praise to keep up its confidence.

To teach the 'down to the sit', hold the lead in the right hand, slide your right foot in front of the dog's paws, pushing them gently back at the same time using the left hand to pull the lead back and up behind the dog's head to give a lifting action. The command 'sit' must be given. This should be practised until the dog is working without help.

To teach the 'sit to stand', start by holding the lead in the right hand above the dog's head. Slide the left foot gently under the dog's middle, lifting the animal, and following this action by easing the lead backwards with the left hand.

The 'stand to sit' should be taught by holding the lead in the right hand, and using the left hand to bring the lead behind the dog's head. Push the right foot up to the dog's front paws and give the command 'sit'. The dog should move back a pace in sitting.

Teach the 'down to stand' as follows. Hold the lead in the right hand and with the left hand move the lead up and back, moving the right foot against the dog's front paws as you do so, whilst the left foot slides into the dog's middle to urge it into the stand position. The command 'stand' must be given.

Practice all these moves patiently until you are satisfied each is being performed happily by the dog before attempting to move away from the

Left: The dog is allowed some time to select the scented item before picking it up and returning.

dog's side. Do not rush this series of moves.

Once the dog is working well on-lead, the exercise can be performed off-lead. Step in front of the dog and repeat the commands, then slowly increase the distance between yourself and the dog until you are six, and then 10, paces away.

Advanced heelwork

This exercise involves off the lead heelwork at a fast and a slow pace, and may include left about turns and figures-of-eight. During the exercise the dog is required to respond to the commands of 'sit', 'down' or 'stand', in any order, whilst the handler continues to move forward.

As this is only performed in higher competitions, beginners are advised to wait until they are winning their

way through the classes before attempting this exercise. If taught too early there is a danger of the dog anticipating the commands and slowing down in the heelwork.

The exercise is taught by taking one command at a time, the handler giving the command and stopping with the dog to see that the correct position is taken up. The handler walks round the dog, then stops again in order to get the dog to proceed. Each position should be practised until the dog is confident. Eventually, it will not be necessary for the handler to stop and circle round the dog. And soon, all the positions can be practised together. Timing of command is critical for this exercise — commands must be given at the exact moment you want the dog to stop.

Heelwork: Turning Right and Left

When teaching turning exercises, the handler must keep the dog close to heel with the constant use of lead and chain, and continuous encouragement using the word 'close'.

AGGRESSION IN DOGS

Before advice can be given on controlling aggression in dogs it is first important to understand a dog's behavioural pattern. The dog, in the wild, is essentially a pack animal. The leader of that pack is the dog that, through brute strength, has proved its supremacy over its fellows. Even in the domestic situation those who keep a number of dogs soon get to recognize the pecking order; there is the boss dog, the second boss dog and so on. Such a system is nature's way of ensuring that the fittest of the species are bred from.

There are also unwritten rules within the pack. An adult dog is very unlikely to attack a puppy or an old weak dog, and will rarely attack a bitch. Two bitches, on the other hand, may be serious contenders.

The boss dog is treated with respect by the rest of the pack, even to the extent that members of the pack will keep their distance while the boss stands over a food dish, almost daring them to come forward. Similarly, it is not uncommon to witness a boss dog stand and intimidate a nervous dog, lower in the pecking order, by sheer presence alone, causing the latter to give up its position on a bed or cushion that the boss dog covets, and literally go and stand in a corner.

Having established, therefore, that there is in the dog a desire for dominance, it is essential that this instinct is not allowed to predominate when you bring home a companion dog, because one will always assume dominance. In other words, the dog must not be allowed to take over the dominant role, whereby the owner lives in nervous apprehension of the animal, and visitors are greeted with barred teeth. Such a situation is serious enough in the case of smaller breeds but can be positively dangerous in the case of larger, stronger breeds.

Below: With two or more dogs, one will always assume dominance—a natural trait that stems from the dog's history as a pack animal and a way of ensuring that the fittest of the species breeds.

The human pack leader

Aggression in the pet dog should be eliminated from puppyhood, before a serious problem develops. While the sight of a puppy guarding its toy or bone may hold a certain charm, this same behaviour in the adult dog could prove dangerous. Imagine, for instance, a young child trying to take away a large juicy bone from an aggressive German Shepherd Dog!

Animals have a facility for detecting nervousness in humans. Because dogs are accustomed to obeying the dictates of a leader, human nervousness instils in them a sense of insecurity which, in turn, can lead to unacceptable behaviour. Therefore, once you have established the role of pack leader the relationship will be a more enjoyable one for you both.

Conversely, it is not advisable to be over protective of a dog. For instance, it is unnecessary to pick up your pet or cross to the other side of the street whenever you glimpse another animal in order to avoid a confrontation. By doing this you are merely convincing your dog that the other animal is an enemy. This will cause the pet to adopt a protective attitude towards you, with the result that it will make a noisy and vigorous attempt to get to, and make short work of, any supposed aggressor.

Controlling aggression

How then should you curb the beginnings of aggression and cope with the occasional fight?

As in humans, there is variance in the canine intelligence quotient and in the dog's nervous reaction. Therefore, while with one dog the firmly voiced 'no', or the banging of a rolled up newspaper on the table, may be sufficient to make it instantly stop what it is doing (for instance, barking excessively or holding on to a bone and snarling), it may be necessary to put another dog firmly in its place—in other words, to put it in a position that is subservient to you by proving that you are the leader. You can do this by firmly shaking the animal by the scruff of the neck, looking at it unflinchingly while you do so.

Dog fights can also prove a problem. When a dog fight cannot be averted by a quick jerk of the lead, it may be necessary to throw a coat over the opponents, putting the animals temporarily off guard, so that you may quickly grab your animal from the rear. Cold water, if it is available, can also have the effect of dampening the combattants' fervour.

The need for self expression

While the excessive barker is a menace that must be controlled, the instinct to give a warning is a natural and useful one; it is the dog's way of attracting your attention for a number of reasons. There is a difference, however, between a reminding bark at mealtimes or a warning when an intruder comes into the home and incessant yapping or barking for no reason at all.

Under extreme circumstances it is possible to have a dog's vocal chords removed, but this is definitely not recommended; a dog, like ourselves, has need to express itself. It is far better that a dog is taught from the onset when it should and should not bark, in other words, it must be taught to 'speak' on command and to 'be quiet' when commanded. In order to teach the latter, it is important that the dog first understand the former. This should not be difficult. Next time your dog barks, you should praise it and give plenty of encouragement: 'Are you speaking, Jess?', 'Speak, Jess, Speak!' After a moment, raise your index finger, and give the command 'no' or 'be quiet' in a firm voice, making sure that the silence is achieved. Then, after a reasonable period, you can ask the dog to speak again until it will automatically 'speak' or 'be quiet' on command.

Punishment

It was mentioned earlier that the dog which, on returning belatedly to its owner following a run, is rewarded with a severe reprimand or even a slap, will in future be less likely to respond to recall. This happens because the dog does not understand the real reason why it

Above: A dog being corrected for jumping up is made to sit and is given a verbal chastisement.

is receiving punishment. It can only assume the displeasure is associated with its own return. Similarly, if a puppy has chewed up one of your slippers in your absence, it will not understand its admonishment upon your return when it happily rushes forward to greet you. A dog must only be reprimanded at the *moment* of wrongdoing. It understands displeasure from the tone of your voice, and similarly praise and encouragement. When it does wrong, it must be left in no doubt of your feelings. Praise instantly when

it stops off digging, chewing or whatever it was that caused your annoyance. It is in the dog's nature to want to please, not to offend. You must, therefore, never hit a dog. If a good telling off is required, a severe shake accompanied by the words 'no, bad boy' should be sufficient.

Remember also that dogs, like people, have a varying range of sensitivity and that just as one child may take a spanking in its stride and another become emotionally upset, there are those dogs which will go to any lengths to achieve their objective, regardless of chastisement, and others which will flinch at the mere sight of an uplifted hand.

Bad habits

There are a number of other bad habits which are likely to evoke displeasure and which should be dealt with in varying ways. One is the habit, particularly in the young bitch, of relieving herself whenever she greets you. This does not warrant punishment and on no account should any be given. Urination is the result of excitement. It is also a normal act of submission. In some bitches it is hard to eradicate, the best course being simply to ignore the bitch until she has got over her initial excitement.

Another annoying habit is that of young dogs who attempt to mount you, or your visitor's, leg in sex play. This act of sex play is normal adolescent behaviour which only needs simple correction. When it occurs, you should lift up your knee, say 'no' forcefully, and push the dog away. Providing you show your displeasure from the start the problem should quickly cease. Similarly, dogs that jump up at you or your visitors in greeting can cause great annoyance. This, too, should be corrected at an early stage by raising your knee whenever the dog attempts to jump up, stopping it in its tracks, and reprimanding it with the word 'no'. The habit will soon be broken.

OBEDIENCE TRIALS

Obedience trials are designed to test the ability of a dog and its handler to work together as a team, and it is this element of working together that makes the sport so enjoyable. Trials are organized by many kennel clubs throughout the world and though the rules governing them may vary from country to country, many of the exercises are basically the same — heel on-lead and off-lead, recall, retrieve, sit and down.

The Australian system follows closely in line with the UK system, whereas the American Kennel Club has a more extensive range of exercises which involves some agility, including the broad jump and high jump. The Club also includes tracking tests as part of the obedience trials system.

The United Kennel Club, the second oldest and largest all-breed dog registry in North America, also organizes obedience trials, along with conformation shows and working dog events such as hunting retriever tests and tracking events. The Club is committed towards maintaining the working qualities of the various breeds and tries to encourage the 'total dog' concept — the idea that a dog must not only look good but also work or hunt well.

Obedience in the United Kingdom

The UK Kennel Club established an interest in obedience after witnessing the success with which dogs were trained during the First World War. Soon the Club had organized a series of trials in which dogs performed a range of exercises and were awarded points according to their merits. The basic structure of the system now applied to obedience trials in the United Kingdom is as follows.

In order to compete a dog must be a minimum of six months of age and must be registered with the Kennel Club. Spayed bitches and castrated dogs are permitted to compete but bitches in season are not. Handlers may only use a slip chain or smooth collar in the ring and are permitted to use a dog's name with a command or signal, without incurring any penalty.

There are six grades of obedience tests, each grade representing a certain standard of training and cooperation between dog and handler. The stages are as follows: Pre-Beginners; Beginners; Novice; Class A; Class B; and Class C. Each stage involves precision control during the performance of the exercises and though the exercises are similar for all stages they do become increasingly demanding from one stage to the next, with the number of points attributed to each exercise increasing accordingly.

The highest standard, Class C, is achieved by comparatively few. Each year, at some 40 Championship Obedience Shows throughout the United Kingdom, obedience certificates are awarded to the winning dogs and bitches in Class C trials, and any dog winning three such certificates earns the title Obedience Champion.

In most cases, the exercises commence and finish with the dog sitting at the handler's side, with the exception of the stay and distance

Below: The owner gradually slips the lead from the collar as an initial step in off-lead training for heelwork.

control tests, and the recall for Beginners, Novice and Class A grades in which the dog may be left in either the sit or down position according to the handler's choice.

In the Novice Class there are seven exercises—a temperament test, heel on lead, heel free, recall, retrieve, sit and down. The temperament test requires the dog to be on-lead in the stand position with the handler standing by. The judge then approaches the dog quietly from the front and runs his hand gently down the dog's back. Any undue resentment, cringing, growling or snapping on the part of the dog is penalized. In the recall the dog must stay where it is until called and then respond promptly to the handler's command. The heel free exercise is to prove that the dog will obey the

command 'heel' even when it is free of the lead.

In the Novice Class the 'sit' is executed for one minute and the 'down' for two minutes with the handler in sight. In Class A, on the other hand, the 'sit' is for one minute and the 'down' for five minutes with the handler *out* of sight. In Classes B and C the period of time for which the dog must obey the commands 'sit' and 'down' with the handler out of sight is increased to two and ten minutes respectively. These two exercises are intended to measure the amount of attention given by a dog to a command even when the handler is out of sight.

The various exercises in Classes A, B, and C, and their relative maximum scores, are shown in the table below.

UK OBEDIENCE EXERCISES

Class A

1	Heel on lead	15 points
2	Temperament test	10 points
3	Heel free	10 points
4	Recall from sit or down position	15 points
5	Retrieve	20 points
6	Sit	10 points
7	Down	30 points
8	Scent discrimination	30 points
	Maximum total score	150 points

Class B

1	Heel free	30 points
2	Send away, drop and recall	40 points
3	Retrieve	30 points
4	Stand one minute	10 points
5	Sit	20 points
6	Down	40 points
7	Scent discrimination	30 points
	Maximum total score	200 points

Class C

1	Heel work	60 points
2	Send away, drop and recall	40 points
3	Retrieve	30 points
4	Distant control	50 points
5	Sit	20 points
6	Down	50 points
7	Scent discrimination	50 points
	Maximum total score	300 points

Above: A dog obeys the command 'sit-stay' during an obedience trial, amidst the many distractions such events involve, including the presence of other dogs and audience.

Below: The dog then exhibits a near-perfect sitting posture by its handler. This is, of course, the start and end point of all exercises during obedience trials.

Obedience in the United States

The American Kennel Club established obedience trials in the 1930s. The rules applying to these trials are somewhat different from those used in the United Kingdom; the following is a brief explanation of the system.

In order to compete, a dog must be pure-bred, a minimum of six months of age and registered with the American Kennel Club. Unregistered dogs are eligible when an ILP (indefinite listing privilege) number has been issued by the American Kennel Club and may be entered indefinitely provided the ILP number is shown on each entry form. An ILP is issued upon adequate proof provided to indicate that the dog is pure-bred.

Spayed bitches, castrated dogs,

monorchid or cryporchid males, and dogs that have faults which would disqualify them under standards for their breeds, may compete in obedience trials if otherwise eligible under these regulations. Blind or deaf dogs are prohibited from entry.

The obedience trials are divided into classes or grades of competition. Beginners compete in the Novice Classes. When a dog has won passing scores (170 or more) at three shows, under three different judges, it has earned the title of Companion Dog, and is entitled to carry the initials CD after its name. The next grade is the Open Classes. After a dog has won passing scores at three shows in these classes, it gains the title Companion Dog

Excellent, or CDX.

Utility Class competitions follow. Three passing scores earn the title Utility Dog, or UD. Dogs which have won the UD title are then eligible for entry into the Obedience Trial Championship and having passed all the necessary requirements a dog will be awarded the title Obedience Trial Champion, and will be entitled to use the prefix OTCh before its name.

Tracking tests, also run under the auspices of the American Kennel Club, do not take place at dog shows because they have to be run out of doors and are not, as a rule, considered a spectator sport. In this sport a dog may be awarded a T for tracking, or higher still, the title Utility Dog Tracking, UDT, if it also holds

Above: Tracking in the United States is taught by long-leash methods. This does not unduly restrict the dog but gives the handler complete control.

the title Utility Dog.

A perfect score in each obedience class is 200 points, a passing score being 170. However, no dog can qualify for a 'leg' towards its title unless it has scored more than 50% of the points allowed for each exercise of the competition.

There are six exercises in Novice competitions. If a dog makes a perfect score in five of these but scores zero in the sixth it could have a total score of 170 or more, but will still not qualify for a 'leg' towards its Companion Dog title.

Above: Advanced heelwork in America involves weaving, an exercise only seen in the United Kingdom as part of agility.

Novice and Open Classes are divided into A and B, the difference between A and B classes being roughly the same as that between an amateur and a professional test. In other words, in Novice A and Open A the dog has to be handled by the owner or another member of the family. Novice B and Open B exercises are identical except that professional handlers and trainers can exhibit the dogs.

It is necessary for a judge to give a score of zero to any dog that fails to perform a principal part of an exercise upon the first command, and the judge must severely penalize the dog should it fail to complete any exercise. He will take off points should the dog appear sluggish, fail to pay attention to its handler, or be downright sloppy in its attitude towards the job in hand. Should a dog relieve itself in the ring

Below: The dog can lose many points if it drops the dumb-bell while jumping over the hurdle.

it cannot make a qualifying score. The judge is also required to give credit in scoring for a dog's willingness and enjoyment while performing an exercise.

In the Novice Classes A and B the six exercises are as follows: heel on leash; stand for examination on leash; heel off leash; recall; long sit (1 minute's duration); and long down (3 minutes' duration).

The heel on leash is designed to prove that the dog has been taught to walk quietly at the side of its owner, not getting tangled up, and sitting when the handler stops.

In the stand for examination, the judge will touch the dog's head, body and hindquarters. If the dog sits during or before the examination, shows shyness or resentment, or growls and tries to bite, it will be disqualified and get zero marks. Slight movement of the feet, or moving after the examination, will bring lesser penalties.

The heel-free lesson proves that the dog will obey when free of the leash. In the recall the dog stays where left until called and responds promptly to the handler's command, 'come'. During the long sit and long down the handler remains in the ring, away from the dog, one minute for the sit, three minutes for the down exercise.

The Open Classes are for dogs that have passed all of the Novice requirements. No dog can enter these classes unless the American Kennel Club has awarded the dog the official Champion Dog (CD) title.

Dogs can be handled in the Open B Class by anyone. A feature of this class is that dogs that have won their Companion Dog Excellent (CDX) and Utility Dog (UD) titles may continue to compete in Open B. The exercises in Open Classes are similar to those performed in the Novice Class events.

Only dogs that hold the title CDX are qualified to enter the Utility Class.

The signal exercise in the Utility Class requires the dog to obey only hand signals, rather than vocal commands. The directed retrieve is designed to test the dog's response to its handler's hand signal directing

Below: A Shetland Sheepdog is tested on its advanced heelwork in Open Class obedience. It is performing the figure-of-eight off-leash.

it to one of three gloves placed widely apart in the ring. The judge specifies which glove to retrieve. In the directed jump the dog is sent away from the handler, stops and sits on command, and jumps as directed. In the group examination the dogs are left standing near each other. The judge will examine each dog individually, as in a regular show

Above: In retrieve over a jump, dogs must clear a hurdle on their way out and on their return.

ring, while the owners are some distance away. The dog must not show any fear or resentment of this. It must not move out of position until its handler is back in place.

US OBEDIENCE EXERCISES

Open Class

1	Heel free	40 points
2	Drop on recall	30 points
3	Retrieve on flat	20 points
4	Retrieve over high jump	30 points
5	Broad jump	20 points
6	Long sit	30 points
7	Long down	30 points
	Maximum total score	200 points

Utility Class

1	Signal exercise	40 points
2	Scent discrimination:	
	leather article	30 points
	metal article	30 points
3	Directed retrieve of glove	30 points
4	Directed jumping	40 points
5	Group examination	30 points
	Maximum total score	200 points

Chapter Four

AGILITY TESTS AND WORKING TRIALS

Competing in agility tests calls for fitness in the handler as well as the dog, for the former is required to run alongside the dog, against the clock, while the animal negotiates a prescribed course of obstacles. The choice of dog for this sport is all-important.

Working trials comprise a series of exercises designed to test a dog's breed characteristics, such as its ability to track, search, jump and retrieve. As in the case of obedience trials and agility tests, the ability of the dog and handler to work together as a team is an important aspect of the sport. Tracking, performed both in working trials and in specialized events, is also dealt with in this chapter.

In agility test exercises, both the dog and the handler need to be very fit.

It is only in recent years that agility has been introduced as a competitive sport in the United Kingdom, since when it has also become increasingly popular in other parts of the world. Many of the obstacles used in agility today have been used in the past by the police, the Royal Air Force and certain dog training clubs for demonstrations. Indeed, the Royal Air Force Police Dogs Demonstration Flight appeared before the public to perform agility exercises as long ago as 1948, and subsequently took a tour of the United States.

However, it was not until 1978 that agility tests were first introduced at the Crufts Dog Show, using a method of faulting the dogs and putting them against the clock. With a few refinements, the Kennel Club legalized the sport in 1980 by drawing up a set of rules. The approved obstacles have been carefully designed to maximize spectator appeal and to minimize the possibility of injury or damage to the animal. Indeed, since 1980, there have been no recorded instances of damage.

The schedule of tests approved by the British Kennel Club can be found in full in the club's book of rules and regulations. The schedule includes a list of the various obstacles, such as those used in the 1986 Crufts agility course, which a dog must get over, under or through during the course of a competition.

Agility tests are considered to be a 'fun' type competition designed for spectator appeal. Anyone who is keen to participate in the sport should join the Agility Club, a club in the United Kingdom that has members world-wide. The Club can give help and advice on how and where to train, and also produces an informative, bi-monthly magazine.

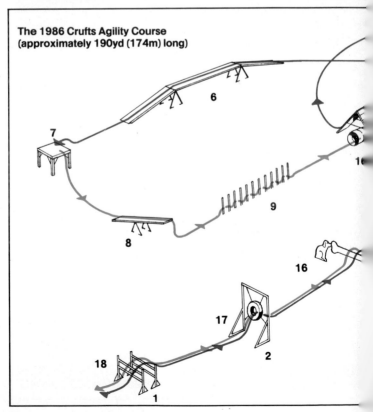

The 1986 Crufts Agility Course (approximately 190yd (174m) long)

Below: The Crufts agility course, which varies slightly from year to year, is designed to demonstrate the dogs' ability and speed.

Above: Here a dog is seen leaving the rigid tunnel during an agility test. Confidence is essential if the dog is to keep up the momentum.

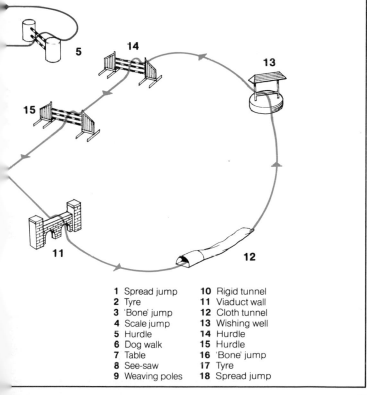

1	Spread jump	10	Rigid tunnel
2	Tyre	11	Viaduct wall
3	'Bone' jump	12	Cloth tunnel
4	Scale jump	13	Wishing well
5	Hurdle	14	Hurdle
6	Dog walk	15	Hurdle
7	Table	16	'Bone' jump
8	See-saw	17	Tyre
9	Weaving poles	18	Spread jump

Agility training

First and foremost, good control of a dog is essential before it can be taught agility. The animal must also be good at the 'down', 'send away', 'recall' and 'distant control' exercises. Teaching the dog to negotiate the obstacles is not that difficult; it is teaching it to do so accurately and consistently that is the hard part. And the hardest part of all in agility tests, usually overlooked, is controlling the dog at speed between each obstacle. This is where the classes may be won or lost.

One way to teach a dog to do something, such as jump an obstacle, is for the trainer and animal to do it together for the first few times until, with repetition, encouragement—and patience—the exercise is performed spontaneously. If a dog is required to jump over a small fence, therefore, the owner, with the dog on the lead, should jump over it also. If a dog is required to jump through a hoop it should first be walked on the lead through the hoop which must be held at ground level. Gradually the hoop can be raised so that the dog has to jump to go through it. If the dog is expected to work its way through a tunnel there must be lots of encouragement from the handler and some incentive such as a titbit after the exercise has been performed correctly.

The procedure hardly varies in training dogs for a troupe in a circus where you can teach a dog to skip by first teaching it to jump through a hoop that is placed close to the ground. Gradually the dog will pick up the tempo and will eventually be able to jump over the rope.

It is important to remember during training that the dog's nature is such that it wants to please its handler. Because of this it is essential that every lesson ends on a successful note, even when a dog is experiencing difficulty with an exercise. If the dog cannot quite make a jump, the jump should be lowered until the dog has been successful, so that the animal can then be praised.

You can begin training by placing some obstacle at the backdoor and encouraging your dog to jump over it, letting the animal know what a

Teaching the dog to negotiate the canvas tunnel

This agility exercise is best taught with the help of a friend. At first the dog will be suspicious of the tunnel, but with plenty of encouragement to give the animal confidence it can soon be coaxed from one end to the other.

Above: The close interaction between man and dog is clearly apparent during an agility performance by the RAF police dogs' display team.

'good boy' it is when the obstacle has been negotiated. But make sure that it does *jump* over it, and not just walk round it.

Next you can make a little fence and jump it, with the dog on the lead, using the command 'up' as you both go over. It may be exhausting for you but is worth practising several times until the dog is enjoying the exercise and jumping readily. The dog should not be encouraged to jump the fence on the way back as this will teach it bad habits that would get it disqualified if performed during a competition.

You should next approach the jump with the dog as if you are also going to jump on the command 'up', but allow the dog to jump alone. The height of the fence can gradually be increased and the exercise practised until the dog is able to carry it out off the lead. Eventually, all you should need to do to get the dog to perform the jump is stretch out your right hand and give the command 'up'.

Once the dog is jumping with ease it is time to think in terms of the long jump, the purpose of which is to ensure that your dog can get over a stream or some other sprawling obstacle in its path. Once again you can take the jump with the dog or, if you prefer, ask a friend to hold the dog while you make your way to the other side of the obstacle. The friend should release the dog when you call it, and you should give the appropriate 'up' (or 'over') command as the dog reaches the gap.

Some dogs have a greater jumping ability than others and it is interesting to note that while sheepdogs tend to predominate in agility tests, gaze hounds such as the

Teaching the dog to jump onto the table

Teaching the dog to negotiate the A-frame

Used in agility tests, the A-frame rises 6ft 3in (1.9m) from the ground. To teach the dog to negotiate it, a second person is required. Holding onto the dog's check collar, lead the animal up the ascent. The helper, standing on the descent side, should call the dog by name and encourage it to come down the ramp.

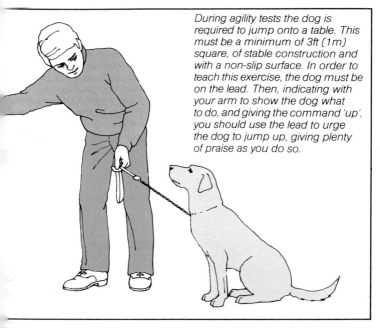

During agility tests the dog is required to jump onto a table. This must be a minimum of 3ft (1m) square, of stable construction and with a non-slip surface. In order to teach this exercise, the dog must be on the lead. Then, indicating with your arm to show the dog what to do, and giving the command 'up', you should use the lead to urge the dog to jump up, giving plenty of praise as you do so.

Saluki, the Greyhound and the graceful Whippet appear the most agile of canines, capable of clearing a 7ft (2m) fence from a sitting start.

The highest obstacle to be scaled by a dog was a wall just over 11ft 5in (3.5m) high which was climbed by a German Shepherd Dog in 1980. Dogs should not, however, be encouraged to overcome such tall obstacles because the frequent impact of landing on the hard ground from a verticle height of 6ft (1·8m) or more can damage their shoulders.

The longest jump on record was achieved by a Greyhound in 1949, when one cleared a 5-barred gate and landed 30ft (9m) from where it took off.

WORKING TRIALS

Working trials are a popular sport in the United Kingdom where they date back to the 1920s when only German Shepherd Dogs took part. Today, any breed may take part, though German Shepherd Dogs, Collies, Labrador Retrievers, Dobermanns and Rottweilers are the most popular and successful breeds. Though working trials are also conducted in the United States, there is far less emphasis on them than on conformation showing and obedience trials.

Working trials are designed to make practical use of certain breed characteristics, such as scenting, retrieving, jumping and so forth, and the right sort of dog is essential in order to achieve success in this sport. Enrolment in a specialized training club where you can be given experienced instruction is also essential. The club will have the know-how to help you train your dog safely and will have the access to the sort of ground needed for searching and tracking.

The following is a summary of the various exercises that take place during working trials according to Kennel Club Rules in Britain.

Heelwork Performed both on and off the lead, this is to test the dog's ability to remain in the correct position. The dog stands on the handler's left hand side with its shoulder level with the handler's knee, and in this position must undergo a series of turns and halts, with commands and signals being kept to a minimum.

Sit- and down-stay Sit-stays of two minutes duration and down-stays of 10 minutes duration are performed, either in groups or singly. The handler must go to the place indicated by the judge until told to return. Meanwhile, the dog must remain in the sit or down position until released by the handler.

Recall to handler The dog is re-called from either the sit or down position. The handler is then instructed by the judge to stand at a specific, given distance from the dog, and on the command of heel the dog must return to the handler at a brisk pace and sit directly in front of him.

Teaching the dog the long jump

To teach the long jump, the handler must accompany the dog alongside the jump, using the lead to control and encourage the animal over the length of the obstacle.

Above: Obedience trials in America include exercises similar to those found in UK working trials, only here dogs must learn to retrieve over a jump as well as on the flat.

Retrieve a dumb-bell The handler throws a dumb-bell as instructed by the judge. On command, the dog must move to retrieve the object, and on further command must return to present it to the handler, sitting in front of him to do so.

Send away and directional command The dog must confidently go away from the handler to a required distance, up to 50yd (46m) according to the test, and may be required to obey re-directional commands given by the handler at the behest of the judge.

Steadiness to gun-fire During this working trial exercise the dog may be on or off the lead while the gun is discharged. Any excited barking, signs of fear of the gun or aggressive behaviour will be penalized.

Speak on command The dog is ordered to speak and cease speaking on command, and may be in the sit or down position according to the handler's discretion.

Agility scale jump The dog is required to scramble over the scale jump, the height of which is determined by the height of the dog at the shoulder—the height being 3ft (almost 1m) for dogs not exceeding 10in (25cm) at the shoulder, 4ft (1·2m) for dogs not exceeding 15in (38cm), and 6ft (1·8m) for dogs exceeding 15in at the shoulder. The dog and handler must approach the scale at a walking pace and halt at a determined distance. The dog is then ordered to scale the jump and on reaching the other side must stay in the down, sit or stand position as previously elected by the handler. The dog should then remain steady until recalled by the handler.

Agility clear and long jumps Except for smaller breeds, under 15in (38cm) in height, the clear jump usually consists of a 3ft (1m) high hurdle which the dog must clear from a standing start. The long jump is usually 9ft (2·7m) long for larger breeds, also taken from a standing start. The handler may approach these jumps with the dog or may stand by the jumps and command the dog to jump. Once the dog has cleared a jump it should remain steady on the other side until joined by the handler.

Searching The dog is required to search an area 15yd (14m) square or 25yd (23m) square according to the test being taken. Three or four articles are positioned in the area and the dog must locate two of them to qualify. A time limit of four or five minutes is given to this exercise.

Tracking On the day prior to the trial, the steward lays the track, which may be a single line or include turns. The dog must follow the track and find the well-scented articles which have been left there.

TRACKING

In the minds of most people tracking is synonymous with the Bloodhound. It conjures up an immediate image of a pack of large beasts pursuing a desperate criminal over the moors. In fact, the Bloodhound, whose sense of smell is reckoned to be three million times more powerful than that of a human, is by no means the only dog possessed of an excellent scenting ability as witnessed, for instance, by the drug and explosive sniffer dogs who are used throughout the world to sniff out the presence of drugs such as cannabis, heroin or cocaine and various forms of explosives.

These dogs have the ability to recognize individual scents, and it is through channelling their natural instincts that they are taught to seek out the specific scent that the handler requires.

Dogs commonly used for this type of work include German Shepherds, Labradors, spaniels, pointers or any other bird dog

---

Below: A dog's acute sense of smell and its ability to distinguish between different scents is put to excellent use in the detection of drugs and explosives.

breeds. In the United Kingdom, even an Irish Water Spaniel has been signed on for such duties.

German Shepherds are often used to seek out the elusive black box when an aircraft has met with disaster, and where wreckage has been scattered over a large area; in the United States they are also being taught to act as 'air scenters' in conjunction with helicopter and boat search teams.

The greatest tracking feat on record, in terms of a distance covered, was that performed by a Dobermann which, in 1925 in South Africa, followed a thief over 100 miles (160km) by scent alone.

The greatest drug sniffing dog recorded was a Golden Retriever named Intrepid, which could detect 16 different drugs and 11 different types of explosives. The animal was first handed over to the Dade County Sheriff's Department in Miami, Florida, in 1973 when it was four years old, and it discovered more than a ton of hashish worth two million dollars on its first assignment.

Above: A young, inexperienced German Shepherd, wearing a tracking harness and on a very short lead, has quickly picked up the recently laid scent on the short grass.

Scent trials

During tracking, or scent, trials the judge, dependent on his riding ability and the type of country being crossed, will be either mounted or on foot. Each hunt has a different line of approximately the same distance, a line being the scent where someone has walked and which the hound follows. The senior line is 3 miles (5km) long and two hours cold, which means that followers must set off two hours after the person laying the line has gone.

Time is a factor, though not the most important one. For a hound to become a scent trials champion in the United Kingdom, it has to win the senior stake twice under different judges, the criteria being that it must do the line without any assistance from the judge and must identify the runner at the end of the line.

81

Training the young bloodhound

As with training for other sports, training Bloodhounds for tracking should be a game, though in this case it is a game of hide and seek.

The owner should hide while somebody unknown to the dog holds the animal. The owner then calls the dog so that it comes in search of him or her. Once the dog has got the idea of hunting its owner, the owner takes over holding it and accustoms it to hunting other members of the family. As soon as the dog has got used to hunting people it does know, it is put on to hunting people it does not know. This is achieved by leaving a 'smeller' behind—a piece of clothing, or perhaps a handkerchief which has been worn near to the skin so that it has become impregnated with the person's scent. This is held in the owner's hand and then left at the beginning of the line. The dog's nose is put down on the smeller so that the animal knows the smell of the person it is looking for.

Once the hound understands that it has to hunt a particular individual, the lines can be made colder and colder and should take in bends and go over obstacles. There are also other lessons to be learned, such as freedom from change, which means that the hound must not change on to someone else's scent, and freedom from riot, which means that it must not, in the course of its tracking, chase sheep and cattle.

The dog's instinct to track is there and it is up to the handler to bring it out. Different hounds are blessed with different abilities but few hounds are unable to track.

Equipment

Keen hounds should be worked in harness; it enables their speed to be controlled until they have settled on the line. However, the lead can be

Below: The Bloodhound is introduced to the scent of the person it is to track with a 'smeller'—a cloth recently carried by the track layer and impregnated with her smell.

*Above: The first stage in training a
dog to track is to lay the scent.
The track layer walks over an area
of rough ground, leaving a scent for
the dog to follow.*

*Below: After the trail is laid the scent
is left for two hours to get cold.
The dog is then positioned at the
beginning of the trail and follows the
same route.*

unclipped if desired enabling the hound to hunt free. The harness should be put on just before what is known as 'laying on' – the placing of the scented article at the beginning of the line. This way the hound will associate the action with 'work'.

The harness for a growing puppy can be made from webbing, stitched in a figure of eight, with a buckled opening on the girth and a D-ring stitched to the cross-over point behind the shoulders. Once the dog is fully grown its harness can be made of leather or nylon webbing. The latter has the advantage of being resistant to mud. However, care should be taken that such a harness fits correctly.

The tracking leash should be approximately 10yd (9m) long, held high out of the hound's way so that the animal does not become entangled or trip over it. But it should not be attached to the hound's collar when working; if the dog's head is pulled up it will distract the animal from its work. The hound should be led up to the 'smeller' (which has been impregnated with the track layer's scent) on the collar and leash then the harness should be put on.

Bloodhound hunting
Another exciting form of sport is hunting with packs of Bloodhounds. One advantage is that it does not upset the anti-blood sport lobby. Also, in the United Kingdom in particular, where railway lines, motorways, wire fences and other obstacles make certain areas of the countryside increasingly difficult for foxhunting, hunting with Bloodhounds has an added advantage in that the lines can be laid through terrain which is easily crossed and where farmers have given prior consent for their land to be used.

One reason why the sport is not perhaps more popular is that Bloodhounds are not really pack hounds and as such do not go in packs very well. They are, instead, hunting individuals who prefer to work alone, detecting cold difficult scents.

Above and right: Trails are laid over as many different types of ground as possible in order to test the dog's scenting ability. Here the dog is seen confidently tracking across a stream and through thick woodland.

Chapter Five

SHEEPDOGS AND GUNDOGS

The televising of international sheepdog trials has introduced a new, widespread audience to the sport. But, though training plays an important part in the development of a first-class sheepdog, the ability of these dogs to work sheep is instinctive; even a pup will try to herd anything that moves and will crouch whenever it encounters sheep.

Gundogs, too, have many devotees, which is hardly surprising when you consider how admirably this group combines the role of sporting dog and gentle family pet. Before training to the gun, these dogs must learn to distinguish various whistles and arm signals, and they must become accustomed to gun-fire.

The Border Collie, which has been bred as a sheepdog, will herd instinctively.

Sheepdogs were originally used to drive sheep and cattle to the markets and it was the role of the shepherd dog to herd, to guard and protect. Today, some breeds of sheepdog are no longer used for working sheep. The Old English (Bobtail) Sheepdog, for instance, once known as a cattle dog and guard, is now kept almost entirely as a family pet.

When talking about the working sheepdog, people usually think of the Border Collie, a dog bred for intelligence, speed and stamina. It takes its name from the English-Scottish border region where it originated. To avoid confusion when buying this breed, it is important to state its full name as several other breeds are also called collies, for example, the Rough Collie of American 'Lassie' fame, the Smooth Collie, similar to the Rough except for its coat, and the Bearded Collie which is really more suited to cattle driving than working sheep.

Sheepdog Trials

The North American Sheep Dog Society in Illinois has its growing band of trialling devotees. But the home of sheepdog trialling is the United Kingdom, where trials have been held almost annually since 1906 under the auspices of the International Sheep Dog Society (ISDS).

Each year in the United Kingdom there are four National Sheepdog Championships for Border Collies. These take place in England, Scotland, Ireland and Wales and culminate in the International Championships which are held in England, Scotland and Wales in successive years.

To qualify for entry in a National Trial a dog has to be entered in the society's stud book before June 1 of the year of the trial. The 15 highest pointed dogs in the English, Scottish, and Welsh National and the eight highest pointed dogs in the Irish National automatically make up the team for the International.

The International Trials take place over a three day period in conditions which resemble, as closely as possible, those which the

shepherd and his dog encounter during their work in the hills.

The qualifying trials are run on a 'National' course. Five sheep are liberated some 400yd (366m) from the shepherd and his dog. The latter

Right: In the qualifying trials the dog is sent out on a wide run to gather the five sheep and bring them through the gates to the shepherd. Following this, it must drive the sheep through two further gates and proceed to the shedding ring. Here, the dog sheds two of the unmarked sheep before penning the flock. Finally, it returns the flock to the shedding ring and singles out one marked sheep.

Below: Having completed its outrun, the sheepdog crouches in position behind the flock, ready to lift it and drive it towards the shepherd.

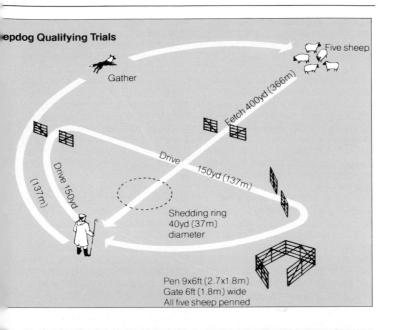

epdog Qualifying Trials

Gather

Five sheep

Fetch 400yd (366m)

Drive

Drive 150yd (137m)

150yd (137m)

(137m)

Shedding ring
40yd (37m)
diameter

Pen 9x6ft (2.7x1.8m)
Gate 6ft (1.8m) wide
All five sheep penned

is directed to bring the sheep and goes off on a wide 'outrun'. The purpose of the dog running 'wide' (on the outside of the course) is, in theory, to shift sheep inside his run towards the middle ground so that when he 'lifts' (moves) the main flock any stragglers can be quickly and easily collected. If the dog were to be sent directly, it would drive stragglers away from the flock.

Having completed the outrun, the dog arrives quietly behind the flock and waits momentarily for the sheep to settle down. It then approaches and 'lifts' its charges towards the shepherd, bringing them steadily in the most direct line to its master.

Once the sheep have reached the shepherd the gathering is completed. The shepherd next commands the dog to move the sheep behind him and then 'drive' them forward through a 'gate' which consists of a pair of hurdles positioned 150yd (137m) away and 7yd (6·4m) apart. The dog must then turn the sheep across the field and drive them through a similar obstacle, again positioned 150yd away. The sheep are turned once more and returned to the shepherd where, within a 40yd (37m) circle called the shedding ring, the man and dog combine to 'shed' (separate) two sheep from the five. Two of the sheep are marked with red collars, and three are unmarked, and it is any two of the unmarked sheep which have to be shed and controlled by the dog.

Once this has been accomplished and the sheep are reunited, the shepherd proceeds to a 9x6ft (2·7x1·8m) pen, one side of which is hinged and acts as a gate. Keeping

the gate open with a 6-ft (1·8-m) rope, he then directs the dog to work the sheep into the pen.

The shepherd has to remain at the end of the rope to make sure that the dog does the major part of the work. Once 'penned' and consequently mixed up, the sheep are brought back to the ring where the dog has to 'single' (separate) one sheep from the rest. This time it has to be one of the two sheep marked with collars. The whole job has to be completed in 15 minutes.

On the third day of the trials the 15 highest scoring dogs compete in the championship event. The course has been increased to 800yd (732m), and the number of sheep increased to two lots of 10. The dog must go out on the right or left side as instructed and gather the first lot, bring it through the gate formed by the hurdles, and return on the other side to gather the second lot. It must then unite the two lots and bring them to the shepherd. Dog and shepherd continue, as in the earlier event, up to the shedding ring where 15 unmarked sheep

Right: During championship trials the dog must gather two lots of 10 sheep, going out first on one side to bring one group through the gates to a fixed post, and then out on the other side to unite the second group of sheep with the first. The dog then performs the triangular drive and proceeds to the shedding ring where it sheds off the 15 unmarked sheep. The dog finishes by penning the remaining five sheep.

Sheepdog Championship Trials

First gather

Drive 200yd (183m)

have to be shed. The five marked sheep are then penned. The 'single' is not performed and the time limit is 30 minutes.

Marks are awarded in each section of the work—outrun and lift, fetch, drive, shedding, penning and singling—the manner in which the dog does its work and obeys the commands being of great impor-

tance. For instance, a dog which moves sheep steadily and quietly without too many commands, but is unfortunate in missing the gate

---

Below: Once the sheep are safely in the pen the shepherd shuts the gate and the dog drops down, still guarding its flock.

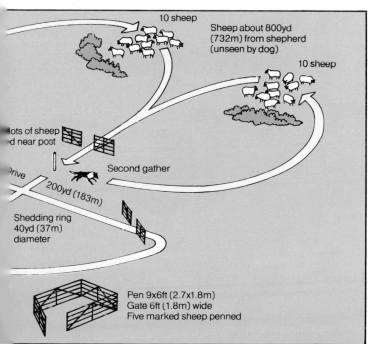

10 sheep

Sheep about 800yd (732m) from shepherd (unseen by dog)

10 sheep

lots of sheep
d near post

Drive

Second gather

200yd (183m)

Shedding ring
40yd (37m)
diameter

Pen 9x6ft (2.7x1.8m)
Gate 6ft (1.8m) wide
Five marked sheep penned

might gain more marks than the dog which gets the gate but rushes the sheep hither and thither and requires a lot of commands. It is the manner in which the work is done which really counts.

In addition to the single dog classes there is a class for doubles, two dogs working together being called a 'brace'. The work for this class follows the same course as used in the singles event, except that the dogs work on 10 sheep and are required to pen two lots of five on opposite sides of the field. The pens have openings only 5ft (1·5m) wide and no gate. The dog which pens first has to remain in charge of that pen, the shepherd and the second dog penning the remaining five in the other pen.

Sheepdog trials are essentially of a practical nature, and the International Sheep Dog Society takes great pains to discourage any freak obstacles and circus tricks during competitions. The sole concern of the ISDS is the practical working capabilities of the Border Collie and its master.

Training sheepdogs

On average the working life of a Border Collie may be 11 or 12 years. Older dogs do not do the same amount of work as those who are still in their prime, but they have the skills of a lifetime behind them and are frequently used to help train the youngsters. The young dogs do the distance work in rounding up the sheep, and the old dog is then sent to bring them in. It will handle close up and do the shedding, which the younger dogs may not do so well.

The Border Collie's ability to work sheep is instinctive, for even as early as three months of age the dog will try to herd anything that moves, be it a sheep, a football or a person, and will crouch when seeing sheep in a field. Some may start working sheep as early as seven or eight months of age but it is sensible to let them come to the work when they are ready and not to rush them. All dogs

Right: Penning sheep is work that is instinctive in a Border Collie even as a pup.

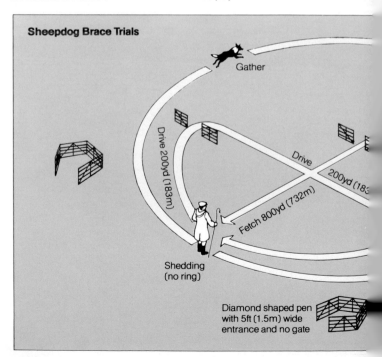

Sheepdog Brace Trials

Gather

Drive 200yd (183m)

Drive 200yd (18

Fetch 800yd (732m)

Shedding (no ring)

Diamond shaped pen with 5ft (1.5m) wide entrance and no gate

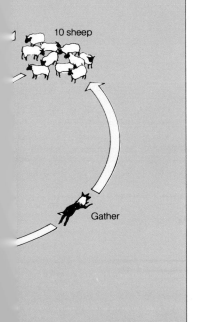

are, after all, individuals and some mature earlier than others.

It would be impossible within the scope of this book to teach someone how to train a sheepdog but the advice given by the ISDS to anyone wishing to do so is 'not to overdo it'. Initially, you should work pups for very short periods of time, putting them round the sheep just to get the feel of them, and teaching them to go out on one side and then out on the other, to bring the sheep towards you and to flank. Voice commands can be used until the dogs have got the hang of things at which point you can switch to whistle commands.

Left: The brace trials is worked on similar lines to the singles trial, except there are two dogs and 10 sheep. With one dog on either side, the brace must gather the sheep and then drive them through the two sets of gates. Finally, each dog must pen five sheep.

GUNDOGS

Gundogs, or bird dogs, are bred and subsequently trained to perform various tasks during the hunting of game. For example, the setter is bred to 'sett', that is, stand rigid on scenting game to indicate its presence and general direction, the pointer to 'point' — by its rigid stance indicate the presence and to point towards the position of game — the retriever to 'retrieve' shot game from land and water, and the spaniel to 'flush out' — drive birds from cover — and retrieve. Though each breed is renowned for a specific task, a good gundog will be taught to perform most of them.

The first bird dogs in England that were used for pointing were spaniels. And there exists evidence from as early as the 13th century that spaniels were being taught to sett. The spaniel today is a good all purpose gundog, in its element hunting out rabbits and flushing out game, then remaining motionless until a shot has been fired. Early spaniels, however, were the forerunner of the setter.

The true pointing dogs were originally used to assist hawks and for netting game. In fact, it is thought that the tendency of present day setters to crouch when pointing is the result of having nets dragged over them during this latter form of hunting.

Pointers are said by some to have been of Spanish origin, brought to England around 1713 by soldiers returning from the war following the Peace of Utrecht. Some controversy

SIGNALS FOR GUNDOGS

Arm Signals

Forward	Right arm by side, left arm forward
Right	Left arm by side, right arm extended
Left	Left arm by side, right arm across it
To ho (stop still)	Right arm by side, left arm held up above left shoulder
To ho (with gun)	Gun held in crook of right arm, left arm held above shoulder
Drop	Right arm up above shoulder, left arm by side
Drop (with gun)	Gun held upright in right arm, left arm by side

Words of command

No	Dead dead	To ho	On	Drop	Heel

Whistles

Drop	Short blast on whistle
Name and Come in	Repeated peeps
Look back and turn	Short blast, pause, short blast
Comeback	Continuous warbling note
On	Tweet tweet and hand signal

exists, however, as to whether the Pointer did originate in Spain or was, in fact, produced in England by crossing the Bloodhound, Foxhound and Greyhound. An authority on the breed, William Arkwright of Sutton Scarsdale, England, maintains that the Pointer originated in the East, found its way to Italy and then Spain—where it developed its classic head—and finally to Britain and South America.

The name English Setter is synonymous with that of Edward Laverack (1815-1877), a man who spent almost a lifetime breeding setters and who wrote in his famous work, *The Setter*, 'This breed is but a spaniel improved'.

The setting spaniel had been used as far back as the 16th century for setting partridges and quails. By interbreeding Laverack produced a strain that achieved not only the standard of excellence for which the dogs were renowned in the 19th century, but also the standard on which the present English Setter was based.

Laverack's strain was to pass on to R.L. Purcell Llewellyn who ran and imported setters extensively to the United States and Europe. His strain is separately registered in the United States alone. The names of Llewelyn and Laverack are still in use in Europe today, signifying a dog's direct descendancy from Laverack's original stock.

The retrievers—the Flat Coat, Labrador, Golden and others—the Chesapeake Bay, which is a retriever of wild duck unsurpassed, and the fine Gordon and Irish (red) Setters are all bird dogs whose true purpose is not merely to locate game birds, but to find and raise them in such a manner that none of the shot birds is left behind.

Below: The popular English Setter makes an excellent gundog and a good-natured family pet.

Training Gundogs

In common with the pet dog that is learning obedience the gundog must respond to its name and learn the 'sit', 'down', 'down-stay' and 'recall' commands. Additionally, it must learn to distinguish whistles and arm signals.

In a manner not dissimilar to obedience training the dog should be taught attached to a long check cord so that it remains within calling distance. If, following a signal and the verbal command 'down', the instruction is not immediately obeyed, a quick tug is given on the line. Once the command has been obeyed the dog should be praised. With repetition the dog will, in response to the whistle and arm signal, immediately adopt the 'down' position.

The lesson should be repeated with a wider distance between dog and handler until, even when running free, the dog will immediately drop in response to a whistle or verbal command from its handler.

A gundog should not be introduced to guns until the end of its basic training for fear that the sound of a shot or of shouting will cow it. Getting the dog accustomed to the sound of gun-fire should be left until the dog has gained confidence. Later it must be taught to be 'steady' to gun-fire.

First of all, a shot should be fired with the dog perhaps in the 'down' position at a far end of the field. Once the dog's interest has been roused a shot may be fired a little nearer, with the dog still in the 'down' position, the handler taking pains to praise the dog on each occasion. Having trained the dog in this manner the handler will then progress by pretending to shoot an imaginary bird.

Quartering

By the time a gundog pup has reached 6 months of age it should be showing proof of its ability to scent, that is, to use its nose to recognize both people and objects. It is at this stage that a manoeuvre known as 'quartering' may be taught. Quartering is designed to

enable the dog to drive the game up towards the guns.

As in all types of early training, sessions should be kept to 10 or 15 minutes' duration. Bear in mind that during the time taken for a man to advance 5-6yd (about 5-6m), a fast dog will move 40-50yd (about 40-50m) laterally. Thus, for every 200yd (about 200m) walked by the trainer his puppy may have run almost one mile (1·6km) and prolonged training at such a pace will soon rob a dog of its merry and zestful style. Remember to praise the dog when it performs successfully.

A fine check cord should be used for lessons. This should be approximately 25yd (23m) long, attached to a slip lead. Handlers are advised to wear leather gloves. These prevent friction burns in the event of the check line passing quickly through the handler's fingers. Training sessions should take place in short grass, in stubble or in heather, not less than 6-8in (15-20cm) in height. If the height is less the dog will be inclined to put its nose to the ground, whereas if it is more the dog can merely jump over it.

The handler should face the oncoming breeze and, with the dog on a reasonably short lead, lead it on diagonally across the face of the wind. After proceeding a few paces he should give a double peep on the whistle and guide the dog into the wind, bringing it diagonally across its original path to an equal distance on the other side. Two further peeps and the trainer once again turns the dog into the wind and brings it diagonally back across the path. The whole process is repeated until the dog has learned that a double blast on the whistle is to be followed by a fairly sharp turn about, always facing into the wind.

The pattern is then repeated, but with the dog now being given more freedom on the check cord and being encouraged to trot. As the

Right: A dog should not be introduced to gun-fire until it has mastered its basic training and is confident in its work.

dog crosses before the hander, the handler must flick the check line across the dog's back to the windward side and then step forward so that, following the whistle signal, the dog may be guided into the wind and turned back across the mid-line.

Once the confidence of the animal has increased and, likewise, the pace, the handler will need but to flick the check cord quickly across the dog's back, and move forward several paces to get in front of the dog's beat, in order to get the dog to turn. Having blown the turn signal, the handler will need to move promptly in the direction of the dog so that the slip lead tightens only gradually about the neck, gently but firmly slowing the dog down and turning it into the wind.

This exercise should then be practised with a slightly longer check cord until the dog will successfully maintain its quartering pattern over an area which is consistent with a spaniel beat, approximately 20-30yd (18-27m) to right and left. Thereafter the pace should be increased and the beat widened until the limits of the line are used. Once this has been achieved the cord should be released and allowed to trail free. At this stage some handlers prefer to use a dog harness in place of a check cord to avoid unwarranted tugs on the dog's neck.

When a dog runs so close to birds that they are raised and scattered it is said to be flushing. However, if such a flush occurs when the dog is hunting upwind it is assumed that the animal has failed to detect the game or that it has flushed the birds on purpose; both these reasons are sufficient to eliminate a dog from a field trial.

When the dog runs downwind it is taken that it will not scent the game so easily, therefore a flush downwind does not constitute an eliminating fault. However, before a decision can be made about flushing of birds in field trials the judge has to consider the wind conditions.

Some young, inexperienced bird dogs may flush by drawing slowly into the birds after detecting their scent some distance away, but with practise they will learn the correct distance at which to stand and point game and, in training, it is best that they be permitted to judge the distance themselves.

Retrieving
You should not ask your dog to retrieve a dead bird until you have perfected its training with a dummy, both on land and in water. And some words of warning, never leave a check chain or collar on a dog when it is swimming; the dog might get a leg caught in a loose collar and drown.

Once you feel that your dog is ready to advance to retrieving the genuine article, start throwing a pigeon or a pheasant into long grass in the same way that you had the dummy. In its eagerness to retrieve the beginner dog may grab the offering rather clumsily, perhaps by a wing, so it is best in the early stages to tie the wings of the bird to its body or secure them with a rubber band.

The exercise should be repeated until the retriever has learned to roll the bird over and pick it up correctly. Otherwise it may have to literally stop and start in its retrieve as it tries to reposition the bird in its mouth, or tries to get a wing out of its eyes.

Do not allow your retriever to go after hare or rabbit until it is obedient to commands. Otherwise in its excitement it may run uncontrollably after the prey, oblivious to commands. A long, single blast on a whistle is used to command the dog to sit and await fresh instructions. When the dog has retrieved successfully, praise the dog to let it know you are pleased.

Above right: Having successfully located the dummy, the dog rushes back to present it to its handler, sitting in front of him to do so.

Right: As with all other forms of training, the dog must be praised when it has retrieved successfully. You should let it know you are pleased with it.

Field Trials

In the United Kingdom field trials take place in the field under shooting conditions for live wild game, fur and feather. The trial, working conditions and terrain are those appropriate to the game, the season of the year and the breed of gundog. Birds are free and the conditions are those that would be

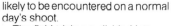

Left and above: The dog returns directly to the handler and presents the bird, holding it in its mouth rather than dropping it.

likely to be encountered on a normal day's shoot.

The field trials are divided into three main sections: pointers and setters, with a sub section for the German Short haired Pointer and other similar all purpose breeds which have trials of their own; retrievers; and spaniels. All of these sections have separate functions to perform and have separate trials run under the requisite Kennel Club Rules and procedure.

In America, hunters, guns and spectators are usually mounted because the dogs hunt in taller cover than in the United Kingdom.

The American Kennel Club licenses four separate categories of field trials all of which are designed to test a dog's ability to carry out the job for which it was bred. Rules are different for each of the groups which are as follows: hounds in packs or pairs chase rabbits and hares; pointing breeds stop, point and permit the hunter to flush out game birds; retrievers fetch shot game from water and land; and spaniels flush game and retrieve.

Chapter Six

SHOWING YOUR DOG

To spectators at any large dog show the art of exhibiting may seem easy and they may wonder why the judge selected a particular animal. Every breed has a standard of perfection, and it is the exhibit which conforms most exactly to that requirement that is selected the winner by the judge. There is more to exhibiting than walking a dog in the ring. The exhibitor must prepare the dog beforehand and know how to present it to its best advantage. Exhibiting involves a great deal of time spent on grooming, handling and travel, and exhibitors often take great pains to become established in their own breed, devoting several years to taking a good example to the top.

Most owners try and make their dog as comfortable as possible during a show.

The proud owners of healthy, obedient dogs may well decide to try their luck at showing. If so, they will soon find themselves competing with all sorts of other dog owners and breeders. Some, like themselves, may be entering the ring for the first time. Others will be old hands, knowing all the tricks of presentation and how to catch the judge's eye. Shows also differ, from small local competitions for every variety — pedigree and non-pedigree alike — to large specialist shows with many pure-breed classes.

Why show your dog?

Shows are the shop window of the dog world. They are a means for individual breeders to show their wares and get the opportunity to see, through competition, how the standards for various breeds are being interpreted by the judges. By selecting dogs which correspond most closely to the breed standard drawn up by specialist breed clubs (and approved by the national kennel club), breeds are kept true to their own conformation, style of movement, type and colour of coat, eye shape and colour, and temperament. Any owners' interest in their dog can soon extend to an interest in the breed, and then into a desire to challenge their own dog's standard of perfection against all comers. Showing dogs can become a compelling hobby or, for some, a lifetime's work.

Time and effort

There is no magic formula for producing the impeccably trained show dog or obedience dog. To be successful demands days, weeks,

even years, of concentration so that the owner and dog become a successful winning team. Indeed, you will soon discover that the owner must learn as much as (if not more than) the dog to excel in the show ring or in obedience competitions.

How much time should you expect to devote to a promising show dog? In the case of a large breed, which takes a long time to mature, think in terms of two to three years of heavy campaigning to bring the dog up to title standard. In a smaller breed, you can reckon on two years. But be warned, it is not unusual for the novice exhibitor to 'waste' their dog through inexperience. Professional handlers are sometimes sought as a solution to this problem, particularly in the United States. While many dogs are

handled by their owners in America, many others are put into the care of the professional. A really promising dog to be heavily campaigned will stay with its handler, living with him or her while travelling to shows across the entire country.

For the amateur, there is little more rewarding than taking a good dog to the top. But should business, disability, age, or some other reason prevent you from giving a really promising dog its chance, then the answer must be not simply to ask a friend or neighbour to take the dog to a show for you, but to invest in the services of a professional.

Incidentally, there is little truth in the rumour that the show dog that is kept as a pet will never win through because it is likely to lean too affectionately towards its owner. Dogs that are cloying are those

Left: After presentation of the award for Best in Show, the winning dog, a handsome Bloodhound, stands on display with its owner.

Below: All show dogs must stand for examination by the judge. This young Dobermann is being taught to stand in the required pose.

which are insecure in themselves. Many an uncrowned champion walking the streets today has that unmistakable air of arrogance, style and quality immediately apparent to the connoisseur.

How to begin

As a novice exhibitor you should start by visiting important dog shows well before you begin to campaign. By all means show your pup at small local shows to gain experience, but attend the bigger shows with the aim of increasing your own knowledge.

Watch seasoned exhibitors at important dog shows. In Britain, for instance, you can observe the people who are awarded CCs (Challenge Certificates), the highest award given at a Championship Show, for the Best Dog and Best Bitch in each breed. Watch these same people handling in Puppy and Minor Puppy classes and try to emulate them. Take note of the exhibitor entering the ring with a dog whose coat gleams to such an extent that it stands out boldly against its competitors.

Never be afraid to go up to experienced exhibitors — in quiet moments — and exchange a few words with them. Tell them that you admire the way in which they present their dog, and ask if you may watch while they groom it on the grooming table. Everybody enjoys a little flattery, and if an approach is made tactfully — obviously you must not waylay someone preparing to go into the ring — you can learn a great deal from successful breeders and exhibitors, not only about your own breed but also about many others. You will find that everyone will have his or her own ideas and tips

Take the trouble to find out who the professional handlers are, and have a look at them too. Get to the show early, so that you can watch the exhibits being prepared. Then, when you feel you are ready, enter your young dog or bitch for its first Championship Show.

Breed clubs

The keen exhibitor will inevitably wish to become a member of a breed club; that is, a club which caters specifically for one given breed. The club liaises on behalf of that breed with the national kennel club under whose rules and breed standard (standard of perfection) the breed is exhibited.

Breed clubs are of immense help to the new member, who will benefit not only from attending the shows and getting to know other people, but from learning by word of mouth, as well as from the literature that is usually readily available, the correct way to prepare and present the variety in the show ring.

Acquiring a reputation

It is important in the early days of your show career to enter as many variety classes (those not confined to one breed) at Open Shows as possible. (A dog must not be entered for a variety class if it has not also been entered in a class for its breed where one has been provided. There is, however, no rule that prohibits it from entering a variety class as well as a breed class.) It is in variety classes that you will come up against Best in Show judges, and entering such classes enables the exhibitor to become seen and known. If you attend only your own breed club and breed shows, you will know only your own breed and its judges. But by showing in variety classes, and indeed going to shows and wandering around on the days when your own breed is not being exhibited, you will gradually become acquainted with the judges and be able to nod and say 'Good morning' to those you have come under, so generally establishing yourself in the dog world.

What to wear

It is advisable to dress in a way that will complement your dog. Do not wear black if you are exhibiting a black dog, for example, and do not wear such brightly coloured clothes that the judge is tempted to look at you rather than your dog. Nor, on the other hand, should your clothes be too dreary; you should aim at adopting a happy medium. This you

can achieve by undertaking some pre-show research. If the judge is a young person, you can dress in a more relaxed style, whereas, if the judge is one of the 'old school', you would be well advised to wear something more formal such as a smart skirt or a suit and tie.

Above: A moment of great joy and excitement at the 1986 Crufts Show, the major showing event of the year in the United Kingdom. This Airedale, having been chosen Best in Breed and Best in Terrier Group, then won the supreme award of Best in Show.

Dog shows are often held in country venues and may require a long journey, so it is good advice to travel in sweater and jeans, taking some smarter clothes with you, wrapped in polythene and carefully stowed in the boot of your car. Bad weather, too, can play havoc with 'best dress'. If, on a blustery day, you achieve qualification for Best of Breed with your dog, you will want to be able to change and look the part for the final judging.

Useful equipment

Watching fellow exhibitors at your first few shows, you are bound to wonder why you did not have the common sense to bring certain useful items. The following list of equipment should help you, but doubtless you will wish to add to it as time goes on.

Benching curtains
Cushion
Rug
Blanket and pegs
Fishing net (for protective action if necessary)
Grooming table and rubber mat (where applicable)
Water spray (where applicable)
Chalk block and/or powder
Tissues
Scissors
Damp sponge
First aid kit
Show lead
Advertising material
Pencil and paper
Velvet glove or polishing cloth
Brush and comb

PREPARING THE PUPPY

A litter of pups which has not been touched by human hands during the first few weeks of life may never integrate fully into a domestic environment. It is easy to understand, therefore, that the pup which has not been prepared for public attention, or been 'socialized' prior to a show career, may become so ring-shy that its chances of success are diminished.

The judge may be confronted by a promising pup which, at first glance, seems a deserving winner, but no matter how good an example of its breed, the judge cannot pick out an exhibit which is cowering in front of him, refusing to look up and shaking uncontrollably. Exhibiting such a specimen is particularly frustrating for the owner, who probably knows that the pup will gambol about happily as soon as it is taken from the show ring.

Temperament is partly governed by heredity. Nonetheless, the pup which prior to a show career—and after its inoculations—is taken on its lead to the local shops, introduced to the neighbours (and their dogs) and is sensibly handled by others, has more chance of developing into a confident animal than the pup which has seen nobody outside its human 'family'.

Travelling

During its show career the pup is likely to make innumerable journeys by road. If you do not want the mere sight of a vehicle to evoke panic, accustom it to taking trips for pleasure. All too often, the first trips a pup makes are to the veterinarian's surgery, where it receives routine inoculations. Why not ensure that your pup's first journeys are made for enjoyment? A ride in the vehicle will not then always be associated with having a needle jab. Of course, you must take care that the pup is not put on the ground before it has had its inoculations. Be sure, too, to cover the seats of the vehicle well in case the pup is sick. To avoid this happening, it is advisable not to feed the pup before the journey.

Benching

Your show dog must learn to be benched (placed in a three-sided kennel that forms part of a long bench) for considerable periods of time. At shows, the benching area is usually in a tent close to the exhibition area. You should never leave your dog bench unattended, so if you wish to walk round the show ground you should first ask a fellow exhibitor to keep an eye on your dog.

Benching can also be practised by leaving the dog in your car for short periods while, for instance, you visit a shop to buy a newspaper. Remember always to leave a window open to allow for fresh air, but not to leave it so wide that the pup can escape. Your dog will come to accept these short absences and learn to guard the car—and, eventually, the show bench.

At this early stage it is a good idea to encourage a stranger to poke a finger through the car window, just to test the pup's reaction. If the dog has a tendency to over-protect, it is a warning that a careless show visitor could at a later stage receive a nasty bite. Where a dog is over-protective, make a point of either putting a table in front of your bench at shows, putting some fisherman's net and pegs over your bench to protect it, or simply leaving a warning notice pinned to the bench, asking visitors not to touch. Biting incidents at shows are more often than not the fault of the spectator allowing a child to poke fingers in the face of a natural guard dog, or, even worse, the spectators doing it themselves. The last thing you want, however, is for your dog to snap and have its show career promptly terminated.

At a show you will need a rug or cushion for the pup to sit on in its bench, and possibly benching curtains to fix around the three sides of the bench with pegs. Exhibitors of the smaller varieties take particular pride in setting off their bench areas to advantage. If you take a grooming table to a show, you will also need a blanket and rubber mat for the dog to stand on.

Below: Space is provided at shows for the grooming of dogs.

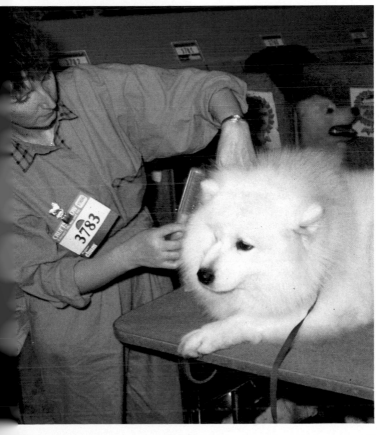

LEARNING RINGCRAFT

A pup may not be entered in a conformation show until it is six months old. But its chances of success will be much enhanced if the handler has prepared it for its show début beforehand. The show dog has to stand still for comparatively long periods in a required pose. It should look as if it is enjoying the proceedings (as indeed it should), move easily and correctly in the ring, behave well towards other dogs and take in its stride a physical examination by the judge.

You should start teaching your pup ringcraft early on by training it to stand for inspection. Smaller breeds are examined standing on the judge's table; larger breeds are examined at ground level. Start by standing your dog with its head erect and getting it accustomed to having its body and teeth examined, prior to being rewarded with a titbit. Then ask a friend to pretend to be the judge and to handle the pup, so that it accepts handling by a stranger as a matter of course.

A judge will approach the dog from the front and examine the head, eyes, ears and muzzle. Possibly he may ask you to show him the dog's teeth, or he may look at them himself. It is up to you to pose the dog, or 'stack' it, on the table although the judge may assist a beginner.

Movement

After each dog has been examined by the judge in the show ring, the handler is asked to walk or 'gait' the dog so that the judge may study its action, after which handler and dog should return to their original place in the line. Small breeds are walked in the ring; larger breeds are gaited, requiring more activity on the part of the handler, so that the judge may adequately assess the animal's movement.

Buy your dog a show lead (not to be confused with its everyday lead and collar) which loops over the head and is secured by a clasp. You should hold the lead in your left hand and always lead the dog on

your left hand side. This allows the judge an unrestricted view of the dog from the centre of the ring. For most breeds, praise and the occasional titbit should be used to encourage the dog to show itself as naturally as possible.

Lead training is another activity best practised first at home or in the garden. For those without a garden, a quiet park or side street may be the best substitute. Practise walking, with the dog to your left, keeping its attention on you. Lead the pup in circles, triangles and straight lines. Pups learn most quickly if their early training is done by one person. Once they are walking well, other members of the family can take their turn. Gradually introduce the dog to areas where there is more activity and noise, but keep its attention focused on you.

Large dogs have their own individual gait, and they should be allowed to slip gradually into this steady movement, a cross between a walk and a trot. The sequence of the gait is right hind foot forward, right front foot forward, followed by left hind foot then left front foot

Above: An Afghan Hound is being gaited in the ring so that the judge can study its action. The other exhibitors remain in line, ready to catch the judge's eye.

forward. Remember that good handlers pace themselves with the dog's movement rather than the other way round; they are also unobtrusive. The judge may be aware of the handler but it is the dog that is being presented.

In the show ring, your dog should always come to a stop unaided on all four feet. This is something you can practise. Move off together, holding a longish lead in your left hand. Come slowly to a halt, putting your right hand out in front of the dog to balance it until, eventually, the dog will stand instantly on all four legs without aid.

This exercise, in common with others, should obviously form part of a pleasurable outing. You should praise and talk to the dog throughout, so that it stands proudly with its head up. Having practised in this way you should then have little difficulty in posing the dog so that the judge can see the full quality of the animal and how well formed it is.

If you have access to a video camera, it is a good idea to ask someone to accompany you to your first few shows to film the class. This will show you the way you move with your dog, and the action of your rivals. Compare your movement with that of the winners and you may see where you go wrong. You can then repeat the procedure in about six months and look for an improvement. If you have eradicated earlier mistakes, now is the time to watch people who are more successful than you and to discover the ways in which their showing of a dog is better than yours.

If you watch seasoned exhibitors in the ring, you may notice that they have a little piece of chopped liver, or some other delicacy, in their free hand. The titbit is used not only as a reward, but for attracting the dog's attention. The dog that learns how to walk and stand correctly, on a reward basis, will quickly learn to look on showing as a pleasant experience.

Stance

A dog is on show not merely from the time it appears in the line-up, but also beforehand. Many judges are making an assessment as you enter the show ring. Therefore, a sensible handler, having already run up and down to establish the correct gait, should sweep confidently into the ring to find a position in line.

The 'stacking' or standing position which a dog must take upon lining up in the show ring varies according to the breed concerned, but the basic principle remains the same: the position must show the dog to its best advantage. Studying your chosen breed in the ring, and consulting with the breed club, should leave you in no doubt as to what is required.

Obviously the requirements in a Novice class are not as stringent as those where seasoned exhibitors are battling for honours. But certainly in a senior class it is important never to let your dog relax or lose its show stance. The judge may, while waiting for another dog to be stacked, turn around and note that your exhibit is always standing there in position. Keep your dog relaxed by talking to it. If it appears to be getting tired, move to the show side of the animal and groom it. In this way you will have your back between your dog and the judge, who will be looking at other dogs. If he looks up, your dog will not be in direct line of vision.

Giving a dog confidence

You should not fall into the bad habit of chatting to your neighbours in the ring, or becoming otherwise distracted to the detriment of showing your dog. Visit almost any dog show and you will see how bad it looks when exhibitors are so busy chatting to their friends, both inside and outside the ring, that they appear to have no interest in their own dog.

It is a good thing to keep in close contact with your dog while showing, and in countries where it is permissible you can do so by leaving your hand resting gently on some part of the animal's body. By running your hand down the dog's back or keeping your hand touching its head or ears, you can let your dog know that you are with it, and this in turn will increase its confidence. (Some countries, however, such as the United States, do not allow such physical contact while the dog is on show.)

Of course, you cannot adopt this practice with tiny breeds such as Chihuahuas because you cannot stand and touch the dog at the same time. But you can nonetheless keep instilling confidence with plenty of praise and encouragement.

Grooming

The breed of dog you choose will have much bearing on the actual time taken in show preparation, but all prospective show dogs must be accustomed to the necessary grooming sessions.

Smooth-coated breeds, such as the diminutive Smooth-coated

Chihuahua, the Staffordshire Bull Terrier and the Dobermann need comparatively little pre-show grooming. Others require more time, such as the Airedale, which has to be hand stripped (clipping would spoil its coat for show purposes) the Bichon Frise which must be meticulously scissored, and the Yorkshire Terrier, which must spend much time with its hair done up in ribbons if its coat is to be maintained in show condition. Poodles, which are exhibited in the lion clip, and the Old English Sheepdog are but two other types of dog which require lengthy show preparation.

Ringcraft classes

Most aspiring exhibitors attend ringcraft or handling classes to learn how best to exhibit their dogs. Such classes are often run under the auspices of a canine society, and it is worth enquiring at your local reference library, pet store or kennels for the name, address and telephone number of the club secretary.

Attending ringcraft classes enables both dog and handler to practise. In addition it helps the handler to learn show procedure while the dog gains confidence and learns to mix with its kind. But bear in mind the different methods employed in exhibiting breeds. The class may not be beneficial to you, for instance, if the teacher is a gundog expert and it is your sole aim to exhibit a Toy Poodle.

Below: Daily grooming with a wire brush is a necessity with a breed such as a Schnauzer. The wire brush is a useful general purpose tool for most breeds.

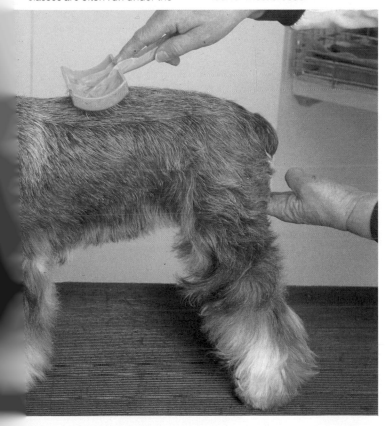

Index

Page references to illustrations are given in bold.

A

Affenpinscher, 14
Afghan Hound, 14, **111**
Aggression, controlling, 57
Agility Club, 72
Agility tests, 72, **72-76**
    training for, 72-76, **74-76**
Airedale Terrier, 16, 20, 23
Akita, Japanese, 30
Alaskan Malamute, 17
Alsatian see German Shepherd Dog
American Kennel Club
    gundog field trials, 100
    obedience trials, 60, 64-69, **64-69**
American Staffordshire Terrier, 20
Anatolian Shepherd Dog, 20

B

Bad habits, how to avoid, 60
Badger Hound see Dachshund
Barking, control of, 58
Basset Hound, 14
Beagle, 14, 15, **33**
Bearded Collie, 17, 23, 88
Belgian Sheepdog, 17
Belgian Shepherd Dog, 20, 23
Benching, 108, **108**, 109
Bird dogs see Gundogs
Bloodhound, 14
    hunting with, 84
    tracking with, 82-84, **82-85**
Bobtail see Old English Sheepdog
Border Collie, 17, 23, **87**
    sheepdog trialling with, 88-93, **88-93**
    working life of, 92
Borzoi, 14
Bouvier des Flandres, 20, 23
Boxer, 17, 20, **20**, 23
Breed clubs, 27, 28
Briard, 20, **103**
Buhund, Norwegian, 23
Bull Terrier, 20, 23
    Pit see American Staffordshire Terrier
    Staffordshire, 20
Butterfly Dog see Papillon
Buying a dog or puppy, 26-29

C

Cardigan Welsh Corgi, 20
Cavalier King Charles Spaniel, **13,** 14, **15**
Check chain, 40, **41**
Chesapeake Bay Retriever, 95
Chihuahua, 14, 20, 23
Choosing a dog, 14-29
    for obedience, 22
    for security, 18-21
    for the show ring, 23-24
Cocker Spaniel, 23

Collie, 23, 77, 88
    Bearded, 17, 23, 88
    Border, 17, 23, 87, 88
    Rough, 23, 88
    Smooth, 23, 88
Commands
    for gundogs, 94
    in obedience training, 42
Corgi
    Cardigan Welsh, 23
    Pembroke Welsh, 23
Cross-breeds, 25
Crufts Dog Show
    agility tests at, 72, **72-73**

D

Dachel see Dachshund
Dachshund, 20
Dacksel see Dachshund
Dalmatian, 18, 23
Dandy Dinmont Terrier, 16
Deerhound, Scottish, 20
'Distant control', teaching, 55-56
Dobermann, 17, 20, 23, 77, 81, **105**
Dog training clubs, 34
'Down', teaching the, 48
'Down out of sight', teaching the, 49-50
'Down-stay', teaching the, 48, **48**

E

English Setter, 95, **95**
English Toy Spaniel, 14
Equipment
    for showing, 108
    for tracking, 82, 84

F

Field trials, 100
Fighting, 57, 58
Flat-coated Retriever, 95
Foxhound, 14

G

Gaiting, 110, 111
Gaze hounds, 76
German Shepherd Dog, 17, **18,** 20, **20,** 23
    in working trials, 77
    tracking with, **79, 81**
German Short-haired Pointer, 101
Golden Retriever, 23, 79
Gordon Setter, 95
Great Dane, 20
Great Dog of Ireland see Irish Wolfhound
Great Pyrenees see Pyrenean Mountain Dog
Greyhound, 14, 23, 77
Groenandaal see Belgian Shepherd Dog

Grooming, 112, 113
Guard dogs, 18-21
Gundogs, 17
field trials for, 100, 101
signals for, 94
training, 94-101, **94-101**

H

Heelwork, teaching, 45, 58
Herding breeds, 17
Hounds, 14
House-breaking see House-training
House-training, 32, 34
Hungarian Kuvasz, 20
Hungarian Puli, 20

I

International Sheep Dog Society (ISDS)
88, 93
Irish Greyhound see Irish Wolfhound 95
Irish Setter, 95
Irish Water Spaniel, 81
Irish Wolfhound, 14, 20
ISDS see International Sheep Dog
Society

J

Jack Russell Terrier, **16**
Japanese Akita, 20
Jumping, teaching, 74-77, **76**

K

Keeshond, 23
Kennel Club
agility tests, 77
obedience trials, 60-62
King Charles Spaniel, 14, **15**
Komondor, 20
Kuvasz, Hungarian, 20

L

Labrador Retriever, 22, **22**, 23, 80, 95
Laekenois see Belgian Shepherd Dog
Leads
training, 34
Leonberger, 20, 23

M

Malinois see Belgian Shepherd Dog
Maremma Sheepdog, 20
Mastiff, 17, 20, **21**
Miniature Pinscher, 14
Mongrels, 24-26

N

Naming a dog, 32
National Sheepdog Championships
88-92
Newfoundland, 20
Non-sporting breeds
in US show system, 17
North American Sheepdog Society, 88
Norwegian Buhund, 23

O

Obedience trials
in the UK, 60-63, **60-63**
in the USA, 64-69, **64-69**
suitable breeds for, 22
training for, 38-69, **38-69**

P, Q

Pack instinct, 32, 57, **57**
Papillon, 23
Pekingese, 14
Pembroke Welsh Corgi, 20
Picardy see Briard
Pit Bull Terrier see American
Staffordshire Terrier
Pointer, 17, 23, 80, 94
German Short-haired, 101
German Wire-haired, 101
Pomeranian, 14
Poodle, 14, 23
Praise, 42
Pug, 23
Puli, Hungarian, 20
Pumi, 20
Punishment, 59
Puppies, 26, **27**, **29**
choosing and buying, 26
house-training, 32, **33**, 34
lead training, 34
preparing for showing, 108
Pyrenean Mountain Dog, 20
Quartering, teaching, 96, 98

R

'Recall', teaching the, 49
Red Setter see Irish Setter,
'Retrieve', teaching the, 50-52, **99**, **100**
Retriever, 17, 94, 98
Chesapeake Bay, 94
Flat-coated, 94
Golden, 23, 80
Labrador, **22**, 23, 80, 94, **96**
Ringcraft, teaching, 110-113
Ringcraft classes, 34, 36, 113, 114, **114**
Rottweiler, 17, 20, 23, 77
Rough Collie, 23, 88
Royal Air Force police dogs, 72

S

Saluki, 14, 77
Samoyed, 17, **109**
Scent discrimination, teaching, 53-54
Scent trials, 81-84, **81-84**
Schnauzer, 20, 23
Scottish Deerhound, 20
Scottish Terrier, 16
'Send away', teaching the, 55
Setter, 17, 94
  English, 94, **95**
  Gordon, 17, 94
  Irish, 94
Sheepdogs, 88-93
  training, 93
Sheepdog trials, 88-93, **88-93**
Sheltie see Shetland Sheepdog
Shetland Sheepdog, 17, 23
Shipperke, 20
Showing, 23, 24, 104-113, **102-113**
  dog groups in, 14-24
  grooming in preparation for, 112, 113,
  113
  useful equipment for, 108
Silver Ghost see Weimaraner
'Sit', teaching the, 44, **44**
'Sit-finish', teaching the, 50
'Sit on heel', teaching the, 50
'Sit-stay', teaching the, 45, **46**
Smooth Collie, 23, 88
Spaniel, 17, 80
  Cavalier King Charles, 14, **15,** 17
  Cocker, 23
  English Springer, 17
  English Toy see King Charles
  Irish Water, 80
  King Charles, 14
Spitz, 17
Sporting breeds in US show system, 17
Springer Spaniel, 23
  English, 17
Staffordshire Bull Terrier, 20

T

Teckel see Dachshund
Terrier, 16
  Airedale, 16, 20, 23
  American Staffordshire, 20
  Bull, 20, 23
  Jack Russell, **16**
  Scottish, 16
  Staffordshire Bull, 20
  Yorkshire, 16
Tervueren see Belgian Shepherd Dog
Toy breeds, 14
Tracking, 80-84, **80-84**
  equipment for, 82, 84
  training for, **81,** 82, 83, **83,** 84, **84**
Training
  agility, 72-77, **72-77**
  basic rules of, 42
  classes and clubs, 34, 36, **36,** 37, **37**
  commands, 42, 94
  equipment, 40, 41
  gundog, 94-101, **94-101**
  house-, 32
  lead, 34
  obedience, 38-69, **38-69**
  punishment, 58-59
  puppy training, 32, **33,** 34, **35**
  sheepdog, 92-93
  show dog, 110-113
  tracking, 82
Turkish Sheepdog, 20

U, V, W

United Kennel Club, 60
Utility breeds, 17
Weimaraner, 20, 23
  Welsh Corgi
  Cardigan, 20
  Pembroke, 20
Whippet, 77
Whistle commands for gundogs, 98
Wolfdog see Irish Wolfhound
Working breeds, 17
Working dogs
  gundogs, 94
  sheepdogs, **86,** 88, 92, 93
Working trials, 77-80, **77-80**

X, Y, Z

Yorkshire Terrier, 16

Credits

Artists
Alan Hollingbery and Clive Spong
(Copyright of this artwork is the property
of Salamander Books Ltd.)

Photographs
Special thanks go to Marc Henrie A.S.C.
(London) who kindly supplied the
majority of the photographs for this book.
Thanks also go to the following for their
contributions:
John Daniels (Ardea London), 97
Roger Hyde, 103, 109
Dr Roger Mugford. 43
National Canine Defence League
  (Marc Henrie): 24

Recommended Reading

The Agility Dog by Peter Lewis, Canine Publications Ltd., Portsmouth, UK

Best Foot Forward – The Complete Guide to Obedience Handling by Barbara Handler, Alpine Publications, Colorado, USA

The Complete Dog Book by The American Kennel Club, Howell Book House Inc., New York, USA

A Dog for the Kids by Mordecai Siegal, Little, Brown and Co., New York, USA

A Dog of Your Own by Joan Palmer, Salamander Books Ltd., UK

Dog Problems by Carol Lea Benjamin, Doubleday and Co. Inc., New York, USA

Dog Training for Kids by Carol Lea Benjamin, Howell Book House Inc., New York, USA

The Evans Guide for Counceling Dog Owners by Job Michael Evans, Howell Book House Inc., New York, USA

Happy Dog/Happy Owner by Mordecai Siegal, Howell Book House Inc., New York, USA

Hunting the Clean Boot by Brian Lowe, Blandford Press Ltd., Poole, UK

New Knowledge of Dog Behaviour by Dr C. Pfaffenberger, Howell Book House Inc., New York, USA

Nosework for Dogs by John Cree, Pelham Books Ltd., London, UK

The Obedient Dog by John Holmes, Popular Dogs Publishing Co. Ltd., London, UK

Successful Dog Training by Margaret E. Pearsall, Howell Book House Inc., New York, USA

Training Dogs by Colonel Konrad Most, Popular Dogs Publishing Co. Ltd., London, UK

Training Pointers and Setters by J.B. Maurice, David and Charles (Publishers) Ltd., Newton Abbot, UK

Working Dogs by Joan Palmer, Patrick Stephens Ltd., Northampton, UK

Your Dog's Training by Charlie Wyant and Peter Lewis, Canine Publications Ltd., Portsmouth, UK

Your Family Pet by Maxwell Riddle, Doubleday and Co. Inc., New York, USA